ST[illegible]ANA

Using [illegible]r for Writing

CAROLINE DONAHUE

SECRET LIBRARY PRESS

If you have ever gotten stuck while writing and wished for an easier way forward, this book is for you.

Contents

Introduction

"So why tarot?" I get this question every time people find out that, in addition to being a writer myself and coaching others on writing books, I read tarot. It's a funny thing, combining writing, coaching, and tarot cards. My cheeky answer is usually that they go together because I decided I wanted them to.

But that isn't the whole story. I majored in Art History in college and loved the process of looking deeply at works of art, both to examine the symbolism and message the piece communicated as well as what the artist was trying to say through it. When I went to graduate school I opted to shift into Psychology and Expressive Arts rather than pursuing an academic career in Art History. I realized that the psychology of creating was what fascinated me most and, back in those days, I dreamt of becoming a Jungian analyst and going deep diving into the world of dreams and archetypes.

Tarot lives in this world as well, so when I course corrected away from being a psychotherapist into the writing world, tarot was a link between the two. I still loved psychology and thinking about how people worked under the surface, but exploring them as characters and supporting writers through coaching was a better fit for me.

I started reading tarot in my late teens, also in college, and remember an amazing night when my roommate and I offered readings by donation at a community art space and there was a line out the door. I was astounded at what I could see through the cards and how much they helped people.

Life went on and though degrees and jobs and needing to be "in the real world" I lost my relationship to tarot for many years. But in my 30s, a friend gave me a tarot deck that had just been created and was creating a lot of excitement: the Wild Unknown tarot. I fell in love and the memory of the power of those cards poured back in. I started reading for myself and close friends and was thrilled at the results.

I joined a few online communities and courses and became a crazed deck collector. There were so many beautiful decks available compared to when I'd been a student. I could not resist all those decks. But as I kept pulling cards for myself I noticed that I tended to get the same group of cards in my own readings, no matter which deck I used or how many times I shuffled the cards. I wanted to know all the cards intimately and realized that I might have to read for others in order to build that vocabulary.

This became the 100 Readings project. In the summer of 2016, I set the goal of doing 100 readings by donation so I could up my comprehension of the full deck at a rapid pace. It was amazing to read for so many wonderful people. I read over Skype and at dinner parties, in coffee chops with friends and pretty much anywhere there was a surface to lay cards on. And it worked. I got different cards. I saw new associations, and I felt my relationship to the tarot growing stronger and stronger.

And then there was one magical reading that was different from all the others. A friend wasn't sure what to ask about in her reading, but she was working on a novel. "What if we ask about the novel?" I said. She was excited and so was I. Instead of doing the reading about her, I did the reading for her main character in the novel.

The results blew us away. She jumped off our session to leap back into writing and I was spinning with excitement. Why had this never occurred to me before? Readings for writing projects? How perfect. And everything came together.

Since this reading, I have found a few kindred spirits who also read for creative projects. The brilliant Jessa Crispin, author of The Creative Tarot, made a similar discovery and has been reading for writers for a number of years. Her book is brilliant and her deck, The Spolia Tarot, has become one of my favorites in my whole collection. Corrine Kenner also wrote a book called Tarot for Writers, but other than these two pioneers, I realized I was in a new world.

I kept playing with tarot as a writing prompt and character development tool and realized that It would make an exciting course. Story Arcana was born as an interactive series of lessons that I lead several groups through before it became the self-paced course available today.

One morning I was in the shower - isn't that where it always happens? - Daydreaming about my online group program, The Coffeeshop Writers Group. The next 6-month session was starting in about 6 weeks and I was pondering the feedback from the last session. People loved support but asked for more tarot and they wanted to know the themes we would explore over the 6 months together in advance, rather than me sharing them as we worked through the time.

It hit me all at once. 6 months is 24 weeks. The Major Arcana is 22 cards. With an intro week and a wrap-up week, I had my solution. For six months, my amazing group of writers explored a tarot card each week and looked at how its themes impacted their characters, their book as a whole, and the stage of writing it for the writer. Characters, books, and the writers themselves all follow a hero or heroine's journey to get from start to finish.

Writing the weekly newsletters for this course was such a joy, and I knew I wasn't finished with the topic once the course was over. It was clear that the next step was to write this book so even more people could benefit from the amazing transformation the tarot can have on your writing.

I'm so glad you're here.

Let's begin.

Caroline Donahue
January 2019
Berlin

Using the Tarot for Writing

How to use this book

FOR ANYONE who has ever read a tarot book, it is a tricky thing to go straight through, isn't it? There's so much information on each card, and there's no way to remember all the details simply by sitting down and reading it.

It is my hope instead that this book becomes a trusted reference and guide as you bring the tarot into your writing toolbox.

READ PART 1 for the explanation of the method and how to pull cards in order to illuminate and identify the blocks that exist in your project. Then, once you begin to pull cards for yourself and your writing, use the descriptions of each card in Part 2 as your invitation to go deeper into what each card is revealing in answer to your questions.

After connecting with the card to find your own

meaning and looking at the meaning here in the book, journaling in response to the cards you pull will bring the greatest insight over time. Explore what you see as well as the prompts contained here in the book and you are certain to open up new doors and new ideas anywhere you feel stuck now.

ONE THING TO clarify up front: this is not a paint-by-number process. If you pull the Tower, it does not mean you have to burn down the main character's house in the next scene or, even worse, that your project is a disaster. Instead, each card is an invitation to look at the themes and opportunities for your story that it contains. And, let's face it, a book with Tower energy in it promises to be a very exciting read.

I always like to say when crazy or difficult things are happening in my life that "This isn't a shitty day, it's just really good material." The same is the true for the cards. There are no bad cards you can pull for your project, just really deep questions you can ask of yourself and your book.

FINALLY, I've only explored the Major Arcana in this book because I feel it encapsulates the writer's journey so beautifully. If you want to stick to the cards you'll be able to find meanings and prompts for in this book, I recommend separating the Majors out from the rest of your deck and just working with them for your readings initially.

However, ultimately, as you become more comfortable bringing your own interpretations to the cards, you may find that you wish to add the full deck back in and pull from all 78 cards. In addition, I've included recommended reading on the tarot at the end of the book so you can refer to those books to get more insight on the rest of the deck's meanings should you wish to consult outside sources. I do plan to write more in the future, and ultimately include material on all 78 cards as they connect to writing.

But those will be stories for another day. Let's get started!

The Theory and Practice of Story Arcana

AS I EXPLORED the impact of the Major Arcana cycle on the writing process, I realized that this progression of archetypes could actually be perceived on three different levels:

- The Characters in the book
- The Book itself as a project coming into existence
- On the writer's experience and process of writing the book

When reading tarot for your writing, it's possible to consult the cards for all of these aspects of the process. While it was a great revelation for me to do a reading about a character, my mind was really and truly blown once I extended the process beyond the characters to the book itself and myself as the writer of that book.

. . .

LET'S BREAK this down a bit further in the context of the Major Arcana:

As discussed previously, the first 22 cards of the tarot create an archetypal story that encompasses an experience much like the well-known hero or heroine's journey. There is a beginning, there are challenges and obstacles to be overcome, and there is an ending when everyone is transformed for the better, we hope.

BUT IN THE process of writing a book, not only the characters are transformed. As anyone who has ever written can attest, the writer changes, too. I know every project I have taken on has changed me, whether it ever saw the world beyond my notebook or my laptop or not. And even beyond the writer, your book or your story has a life of its own that will grow and evolve as it is written.

The exciting truth? You can pull cards and make discoveries about *all three* of these levels.

SO WHAT DOES this look like in practice? Easy for me to talk about this in an abstract way, right? Here's how you might actually use the cards to move forward with your writing on all three levels:

Let's start with an example: something is not sitting quite right with you about your antagonist. He feels incomplete, like he doesn't have enough depth. You aren't sure what's missing and it's been messing up your writing for days. How might you move through this block by pulling tarot cards?

1. From the first layer – the characters in the book:
2. Pull two cards: one for the character himself and then a second card, which you lay underneath that card for what is currently hidden from you.
3. This will allow you to explore both the character himself and the qualities that are hiding underneath and making him less complex or satisfying to write.
4. From the second layer – the book itself:
5. Pull three cards and lay them out next to each other in a row:
6. The first card represents what the book needs from its antagonist. This will give you an overview of the role your antagonist needs to play for the book to succeed.
7. The second card represents what's currently lacking in your antagonist from the book's point of view. Perhaps he isn't aggressive enough in blocking your protagonist's progress so the conflict isn't sufficiently successful. Or perhaps he's too one note and he needs a bit more humanity so the reader empathizes with him and is drawn further into the conflict. This card will shed light on this aspect
8. The third card shows the key to bringing this

character to life. Look to the imagery and themes of this final card to show you what will unlock this challenge for your book. Look very closely at the images- see children on the card? Perhaps the antagonist had a challenging childhood, or once had a child himself but lost it. Let your mind run wild- all the associations it comes up with help get to the depth of your unconscious, which is where the best material lives.

9. From the third layer – you as the writer:
10. Pull three cards for this inquiry as well, but lay them out vertically, top to bottom.
11. The first card represents your intention: this card reveals what your vision was for the antagonist and the biggest best version you can see of who this character could be
12. The second card is where there is a disconnect. Are you afraid of writing this character? Is there shadow material here you'd rather not explore? Look to this card to see what's holding you back from writing the best possible villain you can
13. The third card reveals what will support you in making this character great. This card is here to show you what resources and support you have beneath you in order to develop and succeed in writing this character in line with –and perhaps beyond– your original vision.

SEE HOW IT WORKS? A few tips as you apply this technique to your own situations and challenges:

- A good start is to pick a card to represent the layer you're working with, for example a card to represent the character, you as the writer, or the book itself.
- As you pull additional cards, lay them out so that the location of the card relates to your question. For example, if your thinking feels unclear, pull a card and lay it up high near your head. If you have a bad feeling in your stomach when thinking about this challenge, put it level with the representative card (called the significator in tarot). If something feels buried under the surface, put the card below the significator.

THE BEST POSSIBLE result of reading this book is that you will be pulling cards based on your own specific questions and finding the answers in your own associations with the cards.

IN THE PAGES THAT FOLLOW, I've shared my personal associations for each of the major arcana in the context of each of the levels we've just explored. As you read through these chapters, you'll find an overview of each card and its type and then some prompts to explore for each layer described above.

When pulling cards to help you with your writing, first think about which aspect of your project you want the reading to address: your characters, the book itself (or the plot), or yourself as the writer. Once you have this focus, your reading will be more useful. Then ask your question and pull cards to answer.

To be clear, always look at the cards with your own eyes and without the meanings that others – including me– have assigned to the cards. Giving your own subconscious a chance to look at the cards and respond to the question based on what it sees is essential. Your first reaction matters most.

Once you have taken time to look without references, then you can refer to the card descriptions in this book. Each card's chapter includes journaling prompts for each layer so you can explore the meaning of the card and an aspect of your writing.

AND ONE LAST thing to note: these cards are signposts, nothing more. The most useful thing you can do is let them open up your imagination and allow you to journal and ponder the questions they are asking. The only answer that matters, in the end, is yours. The cards are just a stepping stone to bring you back to yourself.

With all that said, let's move on to the cards!

The Major Arcana

ONE

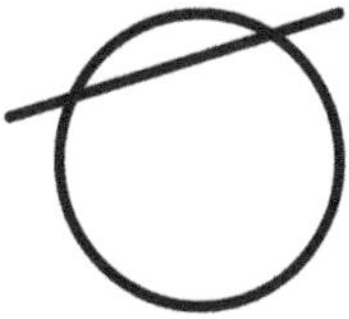

The Fool

THE FOOL REPRESENTS THE LEAP. As you can see in each of the images above, the figure pictured as the Fool is almost always pictured at the edge of a cliff, preparing to leap off, sometimes actually leaping off in the image. However, as you can see, this leap is not portrayed as a fall to injury or death, but a jubilant springing into what's to come.

This is the point when the writer goes beyond saying to herself, "perhaps I should write a book about that idea," to actually beginning to put words on the page. The Fool is associated with optimism, naiveté, but also beginner's luck. There is a removal of the familiar ground to step into something entirely new. In more traditional depictions, the Fool is accompanied by a little dog and carrying a bundle on a stick. The Fool may be leaping into an unknown place, but he, she or they is doing so with support and resources and with a sense of joy and excitement.

. . .

THIS IS the card of new beginnings, the start of an adventure and, I might add, the first page of a new draft. In many ways, writing a book is a crazy endeavor. We spend hours and hours alone toiling away with no clear reward in sight. There is no clear path ahead. Even if you've written a book before, the process is different each time. There are new characters, a new topic, and you're a different person based on your life experience. When we first have the idea to write a book, but have absolutely no idea if it will transform into something worth reading, this is the moment of the fool.

As we see the Fool leaving solid ground behind, it is always with joy. Despite our fears about what writing a book will mean, we can't help but leap.

BEYOND THIS LAYER, our characters have to take blind leaps in our stories as well. At some point they have to leap without really seeing how they will land. If every character planned their actions perfectly and always stayed within the dotted lines, our books would be boring to read, and to write. When you draw the fool, look at ways your characters and your story can take a wild leap into something totally unplanned.

If you identify as a "pantser" this card will bring you great joy. If you are more of a plotter, you may be in a cold sweat jus reading this. Just remember, the fool trusts that everything will be ok and when you pull this card, so can you.

. . .

EXAMPLES of the Fool in Literature and Film:

- Sebastian in The NeverEnding Story
- Lloyd and Harry in Dumb and Dumber

Writing Exercises

To begin the reflection process:

A wise step to take at the very beginning of your project is to keep a process journal. This is where you make notes about how it goes each time you have a writing session. This can be as simple as a few bullet points: "45 minutes in the coffeeshop. Hard going at first, but then it got flowing. Wrote by hand and also typed a bit in the laptop. 4 pm, wrote 600 words."

As you work through the prompts below, you may enjoy having them in your process journal as well. You can also answer them in a regular personal journal you keep, whichever feels better. Use these prompts as jumping off points to get better acquainted with the cards in the context of your writing.

Second, if you'd like to know if starting a process journal warrants the purchase of a beautiful new journal, I say yes. Yes it does. Maybe a gorgeous new writing pen as well- we do need our tools to be ready with us as we set off on our journey. I personally think that a fountain pen and a moleskine or a leuchtterm is what the Fool has hiding in his little knapsack.

Prompts to consider as the writer of your project:

- **Why have you chosen to write this story at this time in your life?** Journal about why this project is important to you. It's important to get clear about what completing this would mean to you right from the beginning, so that you can return to your why when the going can get more challenging later on.
- **What would you like to accompany you?** Who is your metaphorical little dog? (Who is cheering you on and accompanying you as you take this leap?) And what would you like to pack in your knapsack along the way? (Tools you need, scheduling, software, childcare, notebooks, a calendar.... make a list of anything you'd like to have available for your journey)
- **Is there anything that is holding you back from leaping in?** If you feel fear of hesitation about leaping into your project full-on, write it down and acknowledge it. We all have fears with writing, and they are so

much easier to work with if we get them out in the open. Writing can be a scary and vulnerable thing, so give yourself space to feel these feelings right from the beginning.

For the journey of the characters in your piece:

- **What leap does your character have to take?** Whether this is a fictional character in a novel, a version of yourself in a memoir, or the reader who may be encountering your writing to transform themselves, all books have a leap that must be taken. Think about the leap that is featured in your project and make some notes about what it entails, what may hold the leaper back, and the adventure they will be leaping into once they begin. *Note: if you are writing a memoir about your own experience, it may help to give the "you" in the book a different name and think of this "you" as a character for the sake of distinction when writing. Even give her another name that can be edited out later, if this is useful.

For the project itself:

- **Think of our idea for the project as your collaborator** who is leaping as well to meet you in this writing process. So often, we feel tremendous pressure to "make things up" as writers. But what we are really doing, in many ways, is very deep listening to the story that is arising and wants to be told. Try thinking of the story as equally vulnerable in reaching out to you, the writer, to get it down on paper. This may sound quite woo-woo, but I find it really takes the pressure off my writing self to think of being the biographer of a story that's hovering out in the ether, and has asked for my help in getting the story into a book.

- **A fun journaling exercise** is to interview your project and ask it what it hopes will happen once it is written, what leap it is making in becoming a book, and what support it needs from you to communicate clearly with you as you write. Keep these ideas for when the going gets tough at any point later on.

TWO

The Magician

WHEREAS THE FOOL represents a joyful leap into the unknown, the Magician is working with much more deliberate intent. The Magician has assembled his supplies - the aforementioned brand new notebook and pen, of course, as well as several others.

As you can see in each of the card images above, the Magician is surrounded by tools and ready to take action. This is the part of you that doesn't just want to dream about writing a book someday; this is the part that has the willpower and drive to really conjure the book into being.

THE MAGICIAN IS the point where intention becomes action, dreams leave the ethers and come down to earth, and ideas leave our brains and begin to tingle in our fingers and get them typing, writing on paper, or pressing the red button on the digital recorder. This is where you bring focus, drive and all the passion you feel about writing into a powerful point and start the little engine that could chugging forward.

THIS IS ALSO a point of recognition. You have tools on the table. You have been working up to this moment for a long time. This is the point where you dust off your abilities and use them with everything you've got. How exciting! Feel the sizzle of the magician and make this happen now. All it takes is the tip of a pen on the page and go.

This moment comes for your characters and your story as well. What powers are your characters gathering? What are they building up to? What skills have they worked hard to assemble. You see a lot of this moment, not surprisingly, in fantasy stories. A young character learns that he or she has talent and begins to practice and figure out what the limits of this talent is. This is the Magician assessing what the tools are at hand. I personally love stories like this as you can feel the power building as you read.

TO DIVE into the archetype of the Magician, consider these characters:

- Eleven, aka "Elle" from Stranger Things
- Angela Lansbury in Bedknobs and Broomsticks

- Celia and Marco in *The Night Circus* by Erin Morgenstern
- Jonathan Strange from *Jonathan Strange & Mr Norrell* by Susannah Clarke
- Neil Gaiman embodies the Magician both as a person and through his stories.

Writing Exercises

Here are the prompts to explore both as you work on your writing and as you build your relationship to your writing journal. The Magician archetype is there for you both to support you in writing the book, but also as one that may play into the story you are writing.

For your journey as the writer:

- **What would it look like to unleash the full power of your writing self?** If you didn't hold back and wrote with everything you had, what would that look like? Sometimes the most important thing is to know what we're navigating toward. Think about the question, "If I knew I was on the right track, how would I give this everything I've got." Take some time thinking about what your fully manifested writing magician looks. This will help you know what you're shooting for

- **What special powers and tools do you have at your disposal?** You bring your own abilities, life experience, talents, and knowledge to this moment and this project. Give yourself some credit for the magical powers you heave earned through your life, as well as the ones that you showed up with from the beginning. Name your tools. This goes beyond what you wish to have accompanying you on the journey from last week into the talents you have within you.
- **Can you think of a time that you drew on the full reserve of your abilities and conjured something into being?** There are peak moments in life where you pull all of your energy together and get things done. Whether this is finishing a project on a deadline, caring for a sick child when you are beyond exhausted, or getting a dream off the ground against the odds, remember the times in life when you drew on your inner magician's powers. Come up with an example of what this felt like. Know that you have it in you and that you are able to do this again. You are now learning to work magic when you want to, not just when heightened emotions and circumstances pull it out of you. (Examples of this are in most superhero/heroine

stories or any that involve magical powers. See below for some fun watching and reading)

For the journey of the characters:

- **What goal is your character trying to bring into being?** Just as you are the magician bringing this project to life, your main character / self portrayed in the memoir / reader coming on the journey with you is the magician of her experience. The question to ponder is: "What does this person want to bring into being more than anything else?" You may not have this completely clarified in the first draft, but it's something to keep asking about the story as a whole, and in each scene.
- **Ask of each character** "What do you want to make happen most right now in this moment?" in each scene, and for the story as a whole. Even minor figures in a book are the main character in their own world and they all want something specific to happen. If you get stuck, this is a great question to ask, because two characters who want conflicting things can make for a lively scene. Sometimes, you even get one character who doesn't realize she is working for two opposing goals at once. Don't be alarmed if you get more than one answer to this

question. Characters that are complicated are fascinating and fun to explore.

For the project itself:

- **Writing is its own kind of spell.** In many ways, the Magician is a brilliant metaphor for the writer. He's set up with all his tools and ready to cast a spell. The project you are creating is your spell and your tools are your ideas, your insights, language, and all the other powers you listed from above. The way a spell is cast by a magician is that a ritual is performed, and then magic happens. There is still a bit of mystery in here. So assemble your tools, get clear about your intention, and cast your spell by writing your story, and then remember that it will take on a life of its own. A good spell is one that extends beyond your control eventually. Get excited to watch your story come to life!

THREE

The High Priestess

WHILE THE MAGICIAN acknowledges the tools at our disposal, the experience and wisdom we have gathered throughout our lives and can bring to our writing, the High Priestess turns within and takes it a step further: she represents **the writer we already are inside**. Without tools, without degrees, without training, she is the interior writer that lives within all of us. Yes, we celebrated the skills that we have gathered last week, and those are worth celebrating, but it's important to remember that we are writers with or without those tools at our disposal.

THE HIGH PRIESTESS reminds us that we are still writers if we're trapped on a desert island (or in an unending checkout line) and don't have Scrivener, a laptop, our special notebook, or any of our other external tools with us. An old receipt and a discarded eyeliner in the bottom of a purse will get that idea down just fine. When all the tools fall away, you are STILL a writer inside.

By the same token, the High Priestess reminds you that you don't need to read book after book on craft, or grammar, or research forever to know what the story wants to be. Your inner knowing and that feeling of "ahhh.... I think this works" will guide you through the first draft, and the drafts that come after. Of course use tools, do your research, consult with editors and beta readers and other people, but don't let the external trample the inner writer who birthed the idea in the first place.

THE HIGH PRIESTESS urges you to remember that **you** are the writer of this piece. Don't give that power away to anyone else.

TO EXPLORE FURTHER:

- Everything Clarissa Pinkola Estes has written is steeped in the High Priestess. I cannot recommend her audio series *Theater of the Imagination* highly enough. *Women Who Run with the Wolves* is another classic- I recommend the audio as her voice is heaven.
- Byron Katie has a beautiful process called The Work. She is a High Priestess in my life

and her process is profound to do for yourself and to unpack any stuck points you have about "how your project is supposed to look." Her book *Loving What Is* is a great place to start

Writing Exercises

This card's prompts are less directive so that your High Priestess can take the reins.

Prompts to play with as the writer:

- I am a writer because...
- I most feel like my true writing self when...
- What I know is true about my project/story/book is...

For the journey of the characters:

- **What does each figure in the book KNOW to be true above everything else?** Try starting at the top of a page by writing that character/figure's name and then starting a free-write with "What I know to be true more than anything else is..." and let them go on for as long as they have something to say. You may be surprised at what you find. This is great for getting into character motivation. If you ever get stuck and feel unsure what they would do next, this is a great obstacle buster.

For the project itself:

- **What does the story know?** Just as you know things as the writer, the story knows things as well. You connected with the story as a powerful collaborator last week. Continue this dialogue this week as you write. Some good High Priestess questions to ask and free-write from:
- **What message am I not hearing from you?**
- **How will I know when I've made the right choice for the story?** What will it feel like?
- **Is there anywhere I've betrayed my inner knowing** for this story and need to tap back in to myself?
- **What do you want me to know most of all** as I write ?

FOUR

♀

The Empress

YOU MAY HAVE BEGUN to notice a subtle interplay of energy from card to card as we have progressed: internal focus, followed by external focus. The Fool takes a pause within before making the leap, while the Magician assembles the tools on the table. The High Priestess definitely withdraws to gather her insight from inside herself, and now the Empress returns to the outside world again.

THE EMPRESS IS the delicious interaction with the senses and the sensual world within your story. It is also the point when things begin to feel real. This is a fertile moment when things begin to happen. We are moving along in the process now and routines may begin to click along. You've all been at this process coming up on a month now. How is it feeling? The Empress asks you to tune into your body and see how it feels as you write. Does the story tingle? Do you feel emotions coming up that move you? As writers, we can get trapped in our heads and the world of words, but the empress reminds us that we have an entire body that can be part of the process, too. The body can be so much more than a container and transport system for the brain.

REMEMBER TO TUNE in to your body and all the possibilities it contains when you pull this card. The Empress is often pictured in a way that could be perceived as pregnant- see the Dreaming Way version in the top right here for the most obvious version of that approach. This is just as important to consider as a metaphor as an actual pregnancy. We are all birthing writing books and this week, look at what is moving and beginning to live and breath in your writing on its own steam...

TO EXPLORE THE EMPRESS FURTHER:

- Diane Ackerman's beautiful book, *A Natural History of the Senses* is a gorgeous Empress celebration
- If you haven't yet played with Pinterest to create visual board references, it's a great resource.
- Same with Spotify. Lovely to create playlists

and have music that sets the mood for your writing in the background

- Characters that conjure the Empress: Lottie in *Enchanted April* (both the book and the film are favorites), Demeter or Ceres from Mythology

Writing Exercises

Let's look at both possibility and the physical through the Empress.

Prompts to play with as the writer:

- **What feelings come up for you as you write?** Do certain aspects of the piece feel delicious? Scary? Threatening, tense, or liberating? Take a breath or two during your writing sessions and tune in to your body as you write. Does this feel like it's on the right track? Is there a deeper level hovering under the surface? Often the body knows better than the mind that there is more to explore.
- **If something feels a bit dead or dull**, pause and place a hand on your heart or your stomach and tune in to what might be missing or hiding from view.

- A practical question: **Could you be more comfortable during your writing sessions?** This seems like a superficial thing, but often small adjustments to desk chairs, a pillow behind your back or a makeshift footrest can make all the difference between writing for a few minutes and giving up, or losing yourself in a good long session. Make sure your body is comfortable as you write- if you're stiff or could use some fresh air or a warmer blanket or sweater while writing, take care of those needs. The Empress wants you to be comfortable physically, so that you can dream and write freely.

For the journey of the characters:

- **What do the people in your story notice around them in your scenes through their senses?** What do they smell, hear, touch, taste? The Empress wants everyone to get in touch with the physical world around them. As you begin writing sessions this week, take a pause before beginning, close your eyes, and try to connect with at least two senses in your imagination and let them inform your writing?
- **What are the people in the story trying to bring forth through their efforts?** And what can pay off for them as

the story unfolds. Often, people are not successful, or they take wrong turns as they approach their goals, so it's ok if the result is not what they wished for. Just tune in to their actions and the fruits of these actions and how they feel about them.

- **What is each figure in your story's relationship like to his or her body?** Are they comfortable in their skin? Unwilling to admit they have a physical self? Holding their breath all the time? Get an upset stomach when nervous? These details can really tell you about a person as you write about them and it will allow your reader to get closer to their reality. Ponder these questions and see if you instinctively know the answers. I find that often simply asking the question reveals the answer

For the project itself:

- **Engage with the setting of your piece this week.** Try to connect with the senses that are a part of your story's setting. Even if your setting is in another country or another time period, find ways to surround yourself with the senses of that time and place: Try watching a movie, looking at photographs online (making a Pinterest Board of images that connect to your setting can be amazing), listen to music from that time or place, make a recipe from the book to conjure taste and smell, or go to a restaurant that makes this kind of food. Take notes in your notebook to bring the images into words. This is really fun research to do.

- **NOTE: If you're writing memoir or nonfiction from personal experience**, revisiting photographs from the time of the story is a great option, as is reviewing journals to find images and sense details is also excellent- even if you didn't write about those feelings, reading journal entries or past material can bring them back- note them down now and have fun.

FIVE

The Emperor

LET'S do a brief re-cap of the progress we've made so far:

The Major Arcana is commonly seen as the hero's (or heroine's) journey through the first 22 cards of the tarot. Each card is a stage of development for the Fool as he or she learns who he or she is, and achieves that elusive goal, self mastery.

AS WRITERS, we take this same path, hoping to achieve mastery as writers and to bring the people in our stories through this same process. So far we have seen: The Fool as we leap into the unknown at the beginning, the Magician as we take stock of the tools we have at our disposal, the High Priestess where we turn within and begin to trust our intuition, and the Empress as we take in our surroundings with our senses.

. . .

THE EMPEROR IS where we begin to take action. The Emperor is where the plot takes shape. The Emperor is paternal energy in a positive sense. It is stability and order and structure. This is the stage where there is a sense, perhaps of what happens at the beginning, the middle and the end. You may find the boundaries of the project with the Emperor. This is the point to feel grounded. Not just through the senses, as we did with the Empress, but in the concepts of the story themselves.

FOR THOSE WRITING MEMOIR, the Emperor is an energy that can help you define the scope of what period of your life you are writing about. The same with fiction. The Emperor can see what belongs in this book, and what is perhaps the beginning of the one you will write next and can be left out for now.

In addition, the Emperor takes the long view. This is a patient energy, willing to take its time and reflect. The Emperor is perhaps the patron card of the process journal. He likes keeping a log book, getting very clear about things, and having a plan.

In addition, the Emperor moves toward stability and order and away from chaos. If you have felt a bit scattered or overwhelmed up to this point, the Emperor is there to help you get clear and solid.

Writing Exercises

Let's consider ways to bring order, stability and reassuring boundaries to your writing life with the Emperor.

For your journey as the writer:

- **What boundaries, if any, do you need to set around your writing?** Is it time to begin closing a door when you're writing? To ask family and friends to help you draw stronger lines around the time you are writing? Perhaps an app like Freedom or some other way to disconnect from internet and distraction is in order? Assess what you need to protect your precious writing time.
- **What is the scope of your piece?** This is a complex question, and one that can't be perfectly answered when in the thick of writing a project. However, with the

Emperor, we can begin to have a sense of the edges of the piece. Where do you imagine the story begins and ends?

- Let the identity of the story begin to form and use that as a navigating principle as you write. "Does this belong?" is a great question. You'll be surprised how clear the internal knowing can be- this is an excellent partnership you can run between the High Priestess intuition and the Emperor's love of structure.

For the journey of the characters:

- **What are they working toward?** What form are the people in your story trying to create? What are their dreams? What do they wish to make happen in their lives. You don't have to spell this out verbatim in your writing- in fact, it's bet to let the reader discover this as they go, but ask your characters what chaos they are trying to overcome and what they want most to see happen by the end of the story. They may succeed or not, but everyone wants to achieve a certain result and navigates toward this hope.
- **What is each figure's relationship to structure?** Not everyone loves structure. It can feel reassuring and it can also feel suffocating or limiting. Ask the people in your

project how they feel about structure and the idea of order. Do they prefer everything planned out, or do they like a bit of chaos? Or a LOT of chaos?

For the project itself:

- **Do you have a vision of the structure of your project?** Sometimes, it can be fun to play with the structure of your book when it doesn't feel as real as you'd like. Writing a table of contents to post near your writing area can be encouraging as it makes your writing feel more like it's turning into a book. Having a notebook you use for questions that you'd like to address in the NEXT draft can also be a huge help, as it makes certain you'll remember, but that you don't stall rewriting the same chapter over and over. This was a huge breakthrough for me when I figured it out.

- **How is the structure of your writing working for you?** This week, note how you are writing and how the system is working for you. Are you enjoying handwriting at first and then typing in the handwritten words into the computer? Have you played around with Scrivener and found a way to make that work for you? Are you just loving Word and not wanting to give it up? Typing on a physical typewriter? Check in with yourself and the way you are making order of the project through your writing system this week. If anything feels like a squeaky wheel, try some alternatives. Bring your questions to our group call for us to address.

Further exploration:

- Setting up writing sessions on the calendar is a very Emperor thing to do. Play with using a writing schedule this week and see how it feels.
- Prompts are a great tool to bring organization as well. *The Scene Book* by Sandra Scofield, who's come on the podcast (ep. 80) is very grounding and helpful. For nonfiction, there is *Now Write, Nonfiction*. (There's a fiction version of this book, too.)

SIX

The Hierophant

THE HIEROPHANT IS the realm of custom and convention. It is "The way things have always been done here." It is something that can support your characters, smother them, antagonize them, or it can be a safe bubble that they break out of. The custom and convention can exist inside a larger culture, or within the confines of a family, an office, or a relationship.

WHETHER YOU ARE WRITING fiction or nonfiction, there are rules that exist in the space you are writing about. Most people think of Science Fiction or other genres like fantasy that exist in worlds other than our own when thinking of the need to define the conventions of the culture in a book, but these elements are important in every story. Science Fiction and Fantasy definitely have an ongoing love affair with the realm of the Hierophant, but other books highlight this archetype effectively as well.

THIS IS an easy concept to get bogged down in, so please don't use this card to overwhelm yourself. Think instead about how the culture and rules that the main figures in your narrative are encountering impact and define them.

I'LL USE some examples to make this more clear: if someone from your story is traveling to a new place, she will immediately be aware of how things are done differently than they are at home. The differences and *how she feels about the differences* can tell the reader a lot about who she is as a character. Is she scared? Relieved? Enraged? Joyful? Sad or Depressed? All of this can be fascinating to read about.

Another example: if someone in your book is trying to do something he's never attempted before, all the red tape that may get in his way is also an unfamiliar set of rules and customs. These rules and customs are something to ponder as a writer.

SOME BOOKS that use the energy of the Hierophant to create dramatic tension:

- *The Handmaid's Tale* by Margaret Atwood a

dystopian setting and culture that is so smothering that it functions like an antagonist just as much as any character in the book. The show adapted from the book is equally effective.

- *Changing Places*, David Lodge's comedic novel about two academics from the US and the UK swapping campuses for six months has them encountering different cultures and conventions to humorous and transformative effect.
- *The Rook* by Daniel O'Malley, a suspense novel set in a universe just a bit different than our own where the gradual reveal of how the world works to the main character pulls us through the story. Any book where the main character is a newcomer entering an unfamiliar society, city, or culture is making the Culture and Customs a significant part of the story.
- A final example from the nonfiction world: Jeannette Walls' memoir *The Glass Castle* illustrates the breaks with conventional life that she and her family experienced. Their lack of confirming to the usual rules of custom and convention about how people usually live creates dramatic tension in the book.

Writing Exercises

Let's consider ways to explore conventions through this card. These are a bit more complicated to consider, so there are fewer prompts to (hopefully) reduce overwhelm.

For your journey as the writer :

- **What dogma are you feeding yourself about how this book is supposed to be written?** Not only are their customs and conventions inside the book, we may also have expectations around how the writing process "should be done." We have addressed this before, but sometimes looking at the cultural expectations you are trying to uphold in how you write your book can help you see what works for you, and what feels like an obligation to uphold. Let yourself drop the obligation- this is your book and you're allowed to write it your way. Readers will only see the end product, not the process that lead you there so let those conventions and practices be your own. Our conversation on the group call about 'Show don't tell" overkill and the feeling that you're not allowed to use summary is a good example of fighting convention that doesn't work for you.

For the journey of the characters:

- **What are the significant customs and traditions of the world your book takes place in?** This could be a bottomless hole, so don't feel the need to catalogue convention just for the same of writing them down, but it can be helpful to look at conventions that define the time and place that the story takes place in. Is your story about someone who follows the party line or someone who breaks it? Both can be fascinating and in either case, it's important to know what the party line is for the time and place they exist inside of. Again, equally valid for fiction and nonfiction, present day or historical, and our world, or another one, as in sci-fi or fantasy.
- **How does each character relate to the customs, traditions, and behavior**

that's expected of them? Taking the conventions of the setting further, look at how it impacts character development. Do each of the people in your project enjoy living up to expectations, or are they defined by fighting them? Gretchen Rubin's *Four Tendencies* is a great book to break this dynamic down into how people respond to expectations.

For the project:

- **Are you seeing a natural structure for your piece?** If you are still on the first draft, this question may not be relevant yet, but for those of you wrapping up a first draft and moving into a second or later draft, you may begin to see some customs and conventions for your project. Are your scenes feeling better when they're long or short? Do you

SEVEN

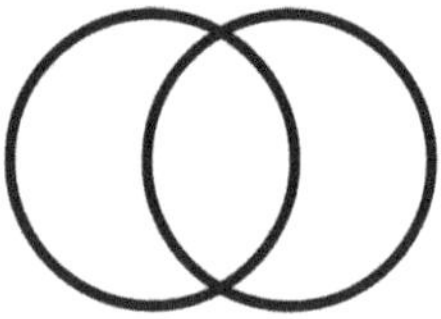

The Lovers

TALK about a loaded card- most people associate this card with romantic love (those of us who played with decks in our younger years kept yearning to pull this card when asking about a crush's feelings), but in actuality, this card's influence extends much further. In every story, there are encounters between different elements that transform them.

This is ultimately why we read- to learn something new and to be transformed as a reader. We may simply want to escape into a story, but that in itself is a transformation as well. This card is about union and transformation through connection.

I ADORE Jessa Crispin's take on this card in The Creative Tarot: that the Lovers represents being struck by lightning by a calling or a sense of something we absolutely MUST do. It is that sense of being grabbed hold of and that there is no turning back. Everything falls away but THIS. I think this experience is represented by the Lovers in how we can respond to an idea or a burst of inspiration like we do for crazy love. The kind of love that makes you chuck everything and move across the world. That's the kind of transformation that can light a book on fire.

ANOTHER IMPORTANT THING TO remember- everyone in your book is the lead character in their own story, even if they aren't the lead in the story you are writing. There is something they each desperately want and are inspired to pursue at all costs in their live. That may be safety and security and so they resist the outside world- not everyone wants to run headlong into a new life. But each figure in a book– even if that figure is a younger you as it is in a memoir – is in love with something, whether or not that love is romantic in nature.

You may not know what it is right now, and it is not necessary to know this for every single person who appears on the pages, but sometimes it's helpful to feel the fact that the pulse of that love is there for each one of them. And to know that if you inquire a little more deeply, you'll find it. I find this reassuring to no end. It makes my characters feel so alive to know they have deep feeling hearts beating in their chests. I hope this inspires you as well.

EXPLORE THE LOVERS FURTHER:

- *Where the Red Fern Grows*
- *Proof*
- *Leaving Microsoft to Change the World* (nonfiction)
- *The Immortalists*
- *An Astronomer's Tale* (memoir)
- *Be Frank With Me*
- If you haven't watched *Fatal Attraction* lately (or ever), it is an excellent example of lightning bolt connection pushed into a very dark place.
- Not all transformations that result from Lovers encounters create happy results. Don't feel obligated to make this warm and fluffy. Let us see the dark side of your characters' obsessions as well.

Writing Exercises

Here are some ways to explore love, partnership and obsession with the Lovers.

For your journey as the writer:

- **What can you fall in love with in your project?** At this point in the process, a bit of a romance between writer and project begins to form. I find, once I have the details of the world in place, I can fantasize about a story all day long. When I get away from my notebook or my computer too long, I miss the story like it's a new lover. It's no wonder so many writers talk about their books like they are dating
- In my podcasting interview with Edan Lepucki (episode 4), she talks about always having a new book on the side like a lover

when working on her current one. For all the talk about how drafting can be torture and that writing is incredibly hard, it's important to find things to love about doing it, too. Look for what you love about your piece this week- this will keep you going when you have to write tough scenes or when you are feeling less motivated.

- **How is writing this piece transforming you?** This may not yet be clear, but we write not only to benefit our readers, but also to transform ourselves as writers. Taking on any big challenge in life leaves you different on the other side. This writing project is no different. If you already see ways that working on this project has transformed you, celebrate them!
- **Make note of what you see shifting in you** as a result of writing. It may be a simple as a sense of accomplishment in getting things written down, or a reduction in the fear that you'll ever actually finish a project as you keep writing. You may still be too close to this to know how writing this piece will change you down the line, but I want to plant this question in your mind so you remember to ask it later. Writing is powerful. Let the impact be felt- it is something to honor. And, just to keep it real, it doesn't always feel great along the way. That's ok. Slogging through mud can bring us to

something amazing on the other side. Love is a powerful force to get you through.

For the journey of the characters:

- **What is the love story of your piece?** This does not have to be a love story between a man and a woman. It doesn't even have to be between two romantic partners or two humans, for that matter. A love story is simple a pulling together of opposites. Like the quotation from Carl Jung above, one of the forces of the Lovers is transformation through contact. What elements make contact in your story and are changed forever as a result? Take a moment to write down potential pairings that create this dynamic: parent+child, character+setting, character+animal, protagonist+antagonist, two lovers, current character+character's past, current character+character's future, person+their health, person+society at large. Any paring that is drawn together and causes fireworks is under the domain of the lovers and worth exploring.

For the project :

- **How can you and your project partner to get it written?** This card is about partnership. We have talked about building a relationship with your project and this is another great time to do so. Sarah Selecky gave great advice in podcast episode 12 about the initial draft being a time of deep listening. You don't have to make up anything you're writing. Think of it as tuning in to the story that is already there in your unconscious or your dreams or deepest self. You just have to get quiet and curious and then take notes. Pay close attention to it. Romance it with nice music, a glass of wine if that feels fun, and try dressing up to write like you would for a date. Your muse will take notice and understand that you are SERIOUS about this project.

EIGHT

The Chariot

REMEMBER BEING a teenager and getting your driver's license? The first time you were allowed to take the car out on your own, without a parent? I'm not sure if every person in the group drives, but imagine that you are given the keys for the very first time, it's a beautiful day and you pull out of the driveway with your favorite music playing and the windows rolled down with the breeze blowing through your hair. Everything feels amazing and the world is saying a giant YES to you. This is the Chariot.

I ONCE READ that there is no card that says a definitive YES more strongly in a tarot reading than the Chariot. It is all systems go, full speed ahead, you are on the right track, now make it happen. It is a fun card to follow the Lovers because this is often what happens when you fall in love, isn't it? You feel the right fit and then you run forward as fast as you can.

Thankfully, we're talking about writing here, so you don't have to worry about a broken heart or being reckless in the same way as with dating. Phew! Once you fall in love with your project, this is the time to write like the wind, write for yourself, have fun with getting as much writing done as you possibly can, like you're a teenager driving too fast and laughing all the way. Think of the parking attendants in Ferris Bueller with the Ferrari. Channel their energy and then sit down to write.

THIS IS the kind of writing day we all dream of. This is the sort of day that you hope for and hope for and when it comes, it validates the whole process of being a writer. So why not try to decide you're going to write like a maniac and give yourself that gift? Say it with me: editing happens later. Write for the joy of writing and putting words down now. Your chariot is waiting!

FOR FURTHER EXPLORATION of the Chariot Archetype:

- NaNoWriMo.org is an inspiring manifestation of Chariot energy, and nice to be familiar with.
- *2k to 10k* by Rachel Aaron was recommended by a podcast listener, and is all about increasing your word count. I really enjoyed

it. Remember, though, that there is no need to shoot for her level of word count. Nano only requires 1,667 words to hit their daily goal. I cannot imagine writing 10k words per day- also, she is a full-time professional novelist with no day job. For me, a 2k day would be unbelievable. I would just ignore the title and take the tips if you read it. The audio version is also good.

Writing Exercises

In many ways, the response to the Chariot with writing is "GO FOR IT!" but let's look at prompts to help you do so if you need a boost.

For your journey as the writer :

- **What would it feel like if you really just went for it?** We spend so much time considering and questioning ourselves and our motives as writers. "Is this the right choice?" we wonder. 'What if I did it this other way?" We can hem and haw and second guess our choices for ages. It's possible to do exercises and plots and spreadsheets and all manner of things ABOUT your piece. But the Chariot encourages you to just go for it and feel the wind in your face as you write like a maniac.

The entire ethos of NaNoWriMo is based on this principle (although I doubt they designed it because of The Chariot or tarot at all). The Chariot encourages you to write as if you have total confidence in the idea and get as many words down as possible. Try setting a timer and writing as fast as you can for that amount of time. You'll have time to edit it later. Just enjoy the feeling of setting aside the critic and writing with speed and joy.

For the journey of the characters:

- **What if there was no holding back your characters really went for it?** This might look like them going full out for the thing that they are pursuing, then reaching out without holding back, or just throwing caution to the wind and saying.a big YES. As we all know, this is satisfying to read about as a reader. One of my favorites that embodies this energy is the book Yes Man, by Danny Wallace. It was later made into a move with Jim Carrey, but most people don't know that the book was a memoir and a true story that's set in London and quite different than the movie in many ways. 100% Chariot and so much fun.
- **What can the people in your book say an unreserved yes to?** This may be a better question to ask if you are writing

memoir or on a subject where you aren't totally in control of the actions of your characters. If you can't be the director as you are in fiction, think about each of your major figures and what they could say yes to with no hesitation. It could be fun to write forward, thinking about what they are each trying to say yes to in each scene, even if these yeses are opposed to each other and cause conflict. A big yes doesn't always make life easier...

For the project itself:

- **What if you just went for it this week?** What if the piece was saying a big YES to being put down on the page. If you envision your project as tingling with anticipation that you are going to WRITE it right NOW, that is the chariot. Think of your project as waiting for this moment where you start to charge ahead and write like the wind. Know that it is thrilled you are writing it and that your story is ready for you to make it happen.

NINE

The Hermit

I HAVE BEEN WAITING and waiting for us to reach the Hermit. I cannot think of a card that better summarizes the writer's process at its core than The Hermit. Most often pictured as a lone figure holding a lamp in the darkness, the Hermit is the part of the process where we need to go it alone and trust that we will reach our destination.

As many of us have fantasized about hiding out in a cabin in the woods or by the sea to write a book totally alone, staring at a beautiful view (I know I have), the Hermit is the part where you sit down and put words on the page without listening to any voice for guidance except your own.

NO MATTER how much you plan a book in advance, things will come up that surprise you. Themes will emerge characters will rebel, you'll realize the story needs to go another way. Sometimes writing feels very much like being in total darkness. There is no sense of how far you are from light on the other side. It is walking across an unfamiliar room at midnight on the new moon with no light to help you from the outside world.

IN THESE MOMENTS, remember the lantern you have with you. The lantern is the thinking you have done about the story. It is your outline, it is what inspired you about writing the book in the first place. All of these things come together as the Hermit's brilliant moment. As long as you keep your lantern with you, you only need to be able to take a few steps at a time and see what's just in front of you. Working this way, you can find your way through the whole draft.

In addition, it's easy to avoid the Hermit when writing. We let other things get in the way, do just a little bit more research, do another outline, or wait for the next writer's group meeting before getting down to the real business of writing.

Can you tell I'm speaking from experience? It always amuses me how hard I fight the Hermit when it's my favorite card in the Major Arcana. it is the point when you believe in yourself, in your story and write what you know to be true without needing any approval from anyone else. It's when you shut the door and get the thing down on the page.

. . .

FURTHER EXPLORATION:

- *Walden* by Thoreau is a lovely example of The Hermit.
- If you need help retreating from technology to go into Hermit mode, try something like the app Freedom, which lets you control when you are connected to the internet.
- Another option is the app Forest, which lets little trees grow during windows of time as long as you don't use your phone.
- Secret Library Podcast guest Ben Percy (ep. 92) also swore by the book *Deep Work*, which is an ode to the energy of the Hermit and how badly we all need it.

Writing Exercises

The Hermit asks you to go deep, avoid distraction, and really dive in. Here are some ways to get the most out of Hermit energy for your writing:

For your journey as the writer:

- **Can you carve out some Hermit time and space this week?** Could you get away somehow to write? Or simply find an evening after dinner or early in the morning to shut yourself away from other responsibilities and interaction and just write? What would it look like to tell yourself that it's time to get on with the solitary process of writing. There is no need to seek any further validation from the outside world now. If you can get away for a night or more, do it. But if now, try to hermit in other places: your bedroom, even the bathroom can be a retreat with a notebook and a cup of tea and someone else watching children or pets or boiling pots. Give yourself the space to write alone this week.

For the journey of the characters:

- **What decisions or actions must they undertake alone?** Is there something your character cannot do with anyone else? Is there something she has to stop avoiding and just settle down to do on her own? It can be fun to think about actions that need to be taken and consider whether having others present would help or hinder the process for your characters or figures.
- **Go through the things your character needs to accomplish** and see if there is anything he needs to do on his own. Or is there a moment she needs to step away from needing approval from the outside world? Let her escape a bit on her own and breathe.
- **Explore what clarity and self-knowledge your characters need to find.** How well do the figures in your story know themselves? How well do they enjoy their own company? Is this something that you can bring them into closer contact with? Do they enjoy being alone or do they fear it? Or even crave it because it is so rarely

possible. Consider what solitude looks like to the people you are writing about and how getting time alone (or never getting it) impacts and changes them.

For the project itself:

- **What is the lantern revealing as you write?** There is always some element of the unknown that you don't have access to until you actually write the book. What elements are still in the dark and which ones are lit up for you right now. Try drawing a diagram of concentric circles.
- The center is the brightest where you are and as you get into circles as you expand further and further from the light, list things that you feel more and more uncertain of inside the circles. In the center you know your character's age, where she lives and what she wants for herself, but in a circle further from the light is why she wants it, the things she's scared of and why she's so angry, and in a dimmer circle still there is a relationship in her family. The farthest from the center, the less clear the material is, to you or to your character. This exercise can work for both options.
- Sometimes a visual map is a good way to lay out the known and unknown landscape of the story.

TEN

Strength

WHEREAS THE CHARIOT was a leaping ahead of gleeful energy, much like a puppy who can barely contain his excitement and does not react well initially to a leash, Strength is a more sustained energy that can hold on for a longer period.

Let the Chariot fire you up and get your moving, but Strength is what will get you through the full process. I like to think of Strength as the marathon, whereas the Chariot was most definitely a sprint.

STRENGTH IS LONG ASSOCIATED with the Lion, usually prominently pictured on the card. Either a lion on its own, as in the Wild Unknown, or in relationship to a woman. This pairing often shows the woman taming the lion and stroking it to calm its wild energy, or in some cases even taking hold of its teeth. One of my favorite depictions is the Circo tarot, which shows the woman wearing a lion suit as a badge of courage.

THIS DYNAMIC, as it plays out in writing, speaking to getting into the deeply unconscious motivations of the figures in your story. What do they fear? What puts them into fight or flight? This is a very animal energy, much like my feral kitten, who started at every single sound when we first brought him home. This energy is more primal than psychological- there is a card for the psychological depths later in the sequence, not to worry.

Think of this Strength as the force that allows you as the writer, and your characters as well, to face your base-level fears. It is Strength that goes downstairs to investigate a bump in the night with a flashlight. Strength is willing to face its fears and to understand them better. It is a grounded powerful energy. The woman in the images knows she is dealing with a lion, but she reaches forward and pets it anyway.

FOR FURTHER EXPLORATION:

- A classic story with characters who embody both succeeding and failing to master Strength is Lord of the Rings. Frodo is the success story, while Gollum is torn apart by a power that overwhelms him.

Writing Exercises

Strength counsels slow steps forward with measured action. Think of slowly approaching a scared animal.

For your journey as the writer:

- **What requires caution and patience to approach?** What aspect of your project makes you feel skittish and scared? After a joyful leaping ahead like we had last week with the Chariot, fear can rear its head again with new niggling doubts and consequences it imagines will take place now that you are writing with such abandon. Don't try to shut them out. Be like the woman with the lion and soothe them. Listen to the fears as they come up - maybe about what people will think, what the work will be like, how your life will change if you share your work...listen quietly and stroke them into submission with a calm and confident touch. Your creative self will become calm again.

For the journey of the characters:

- **What scares your characters? What threat do they perceive in their worlds?** One of the most difficult things to do in a story is to fully connect with your characters, to take on their feelings, and then to push them to their limits, and beyond. If you are a character in your story, the same applies. Revisiting these places when writing memoir or nonfiction can be just as scary. Think about what the figures in your story are scared of, and how you can bring that fear up close to them. Let them feel the lion's breath in their faces. How will this change them?
- **Try a monologue free write.** Take a blank sheet of paper and write "What scares me more than anything is..." and let your character fill in the gaps. When they run out of things to say, add "what scares me about that is..." and then let them continue. Set a timer for 10 minutes for this exercise and see what your discover.

For the project itself:

- **What is luring in the dark underneath the surface of the story you are telling?** In first drafts, we often hover on the surface. We get the characters but not the action clear, or the reverse. Good stories always have something scary in them. It doesn't have to be a horror story- Jane Austen was full of the fear of being left a destitute spinster and that is every bit as scary to those characters as the classic suspense from something like Gone Girl. After doing the exercise above with a couple of main characters, see if their fears below their conscious minds are creating an entire subplot below the surface your hadn't thought of before...

ELEVEN

Wheel of Fortune

AS ROMAN NUMERAL X, Wheel of Fortune is actually the 11th card in the deck, since the Fool begins the cycle at 0. We are now at the zenith of the cycle and, if we visualize the journey as a circle, the Wheel of Fortune card marks the point when we are the furthest away from where we began. As such, destitute orphans to dizzying wealth, and back down into the gutter in the space of one book.

THE WHEEL of Fortune has absolutely no notion of "fair." Despite writing diligently for months, you can have an a-ha moment that shows you that you need to re-write the whole story. Or on the opposite site, you can give up on a project completely, only to wake up in the middle of the night with an astonishing a-ha moment where the entire thing comes together. All things are possible, but you cannot plan for any of them in advance. This is the Wheel of Fortune.

IN MANY WAYS, this card has come to exemplify the sort of book readers love these days- the plot twist. Think Gone Girl or Girl on the Train or the film The Usual Suspects. You follow the story along, thinking you know where it's headed only to have the rug pulled out from under you. The Wheel of Fortune is the rug getting yanked away, and it can happen to you as the writer, your characters as they are minding their own business and going about their lives and, if you want to write that sort of book, it's a curveball you can throw right at your reader.

The Wheel of Fortune asks you to let go of certainty, or outlines plotted too tightly, and to recognize that you are way out in space now, like astronauts that have a ways to go before they get to come back down to Earth. Try to enjoy the loss of gravity and let yourself float now. You may even find things are more fun with you left them start to spin on the wheel.

FOR FURTHER EXPLORATION:

- Dickens, The Russian Novelists, and all of Opera are great examples of the Wheel of Fortune in action.
- A fun way to play with the Wheel? Start writing a scene, and pick a tarot card as a

prompt for what happens next. Repeat through the scene to let go of control of the plot completely.

- Throw a few and make a story or a scene out of the resulting combination. Really fun way to keep your imagination nimble and able to leap into the unknown at a moment's notice. There are many cool expansion packs and themes. I can easily see this being used for science fiction or fantasy, but they would work for any piece of writing with the spirit of experimentation turned up.

Writing Exercises

The Wheel of Fortune asks for a release of control and to let fate rule. This can be applied in three layers, as we have seen in each card up to now:

For your journey as the writer :

- **Are you having swings between productivity and stuckness?** The Wheel of Fortune asks you to understand that you will have good writing days and bad writing days. That some days it will feel amazing and easy and you can't write fast enough to keep up with how effortlessly the words are coming to you. And other days it will be dry dry dry. There is not always a reason for this. We can't always take vitamins, get a good night's sleep, and sip our favorite tea and be promised a productive writing session. But the Wheel of Fortune rewards those who keep showing up no matter what the experience looks like.

- **Have you had a sudden shift in your concept of the piece?** The Wheel of Fortune can also pull the rug out by hitting you with a blast of insight that changes the entire foundation of your project. "Tell it from the other character's point of view." "This character is not who you think they are." Or the one I was treated to once while in Savasana in a yoga class: "Your book is supposed to be in the first person." Oof. These moments can make you feel that the Wheel has run over you instead of carrying you on an entertaining ride. But rest assured, even if it flings you down with one day, it always carries you back up as it cycles forward.

For the journey of the characters:

- **What would it look like for your character to be hit with drastically different circumstances?** What if they suddenly inherited a fortune? Lost everything? Met a long-lost relative? Failed the test that was going to take them forward to the perfect life? Were presented with an offer too amazing to pass up?
- These kinds of sudden shifts push your

characters to the edge and show what they are really made of. In addition, people reading love to go along for this kind of ride from the safety of their own reading chair. If you're writing non-fiction or memoir, what moments felt like this? When did your world flip upside down and how did those moments propel the action forward.

- In many ways, Wheel of Fortune moments always frame big stories. Memoirs are often about taking a big leap or what happened when the person writing crashed and burned when trying to move forward. These stories are relatable and engaging because we all know what it feels like to get blindsided.
- **What is the worst or best thing that could happen to your characters?** This is a bit of an extension of looking at what their fears were, but in each scene or each moment that you write about, ask yourself "How could this go the most wrong?" as well as "How could this go the most right?" Most successful stories are a mix of both happening over the course of the story. If, in each scene, you ponder these questions, it will help keep the action moving.
- You don't need to write the worst and best thing in every scene, as that would be impossible to achieve – although I challenge you to try – but pondering what it would look like can allow new plot arcs to build and

it does allow you to ponder whether it is more interesting or more fun to write if things suddenly go well or collapse underneath the people in your story.

For the project itself:

- **What is the turning point of the story?** We are at the halfway point in the course now, and we are going to start to make our way back. In classic plot terms, we are heading toward the third act. While we are only halfway through the course, endings are the hardest parts of a piece to write in many cases, so we will be slowing way down to consider them from a number of angles. As we hit the furthest point and begin to head home to the resolution of the story, consider what the climax might be? There will be another chance to explore this with the Tower. If the Wheel of Fortune could be a positive or devastating twist of fate, the Tower always signals things falling apart.
- Some of the most powerful stories have an upturn followed by the loss of this good fortune and we feel that loss all the more for how fragile the brief happiness was. Look at Romeo + Juliet, Cold Mountain, Gone With the Wind, and many other dramas to see a brief love or period of joy followed by ruin and devastation.

- The characters have to go through something that transforms them. Sadly we can't protect them from this. And the Wheel of Fortune is when you see the change coming, even if it hasn't hit the page just yet.

TWELVE

Justice

JUSTICE IS the moment when we expand from just he character's lives to a wide view of the entire system they inhabit. We start to think about how things will play out based on the character's actions and think them through until the end. It's when we start to think about consequences and results. Justice is, in many ways, the ruler of endings. have you ever read a book where it didn't end the way you'd hoped, but it felt right? That's Justice in action.

THE TENSION of Justice is recognizing that we all want the happy ever after, but our characters – if they are interesting ones – often make choices that prevent that kind fo payoff. Alcoholic character who refuses to make changes in her life and continues to rob banks to subsidize her lifestyle? Dramatic and silly example, but one that is unlikely to end in a cozy and unblemished scene of domestic bliss.

WHAT CHOICES ARE the figures in your project making and how are they likely to impact the other people they interact with as the story unfolds? How will these choices impact their goals? Their hopes? Their choices? The world around them? Justice is the cold and impersonal side of an "if this, then that" equation. If you put your hand on a hot stove, you will get burned. It doesn't feel good, but it's how Justice works. It's important to know what these systems look like in the world your story takes place in, as well as in the minds of the people you are writing about.

Knowing what Justice looks like for your characters and for the world they live in does NOT mean the story has to follow that path. We love seeing people try to cheat Justice. We also love seeing people seek Justice and can be equally satisfied by seeing them get it and watching it slip from their grasp. You can make whatever choice you like, but it will be a stronger ending if you know what Justice is for the people in your project.

TO EXPLORE FURTHER:

- Both K.M. Weiland's *Outlining Your Novel* and *Structuring Your Novel* are great to start thinking about outcome and Justice will win out in the end, or not. Each book has a companion workbook. If you don't want to read the full books, there's a lot to gain by just working straight through the workbooks.

Writing Exercises

Justice asks you to identify the ultimate outcome your character is seeking. This can be applied in three layers, as we have seen in each card up to now:

For your journey as the writer:

- **What do you hope to achieve with this project?** Do you have a mission as the writer of this project? Is there a kind of Justice you hope to achieve by putting this down on paper? Seeing Justice or having a mission of some kind is a powerful motivator. If you find that you do have a kind of Justice you are pursuing, it's good to know as it can keep you pressing forward when things get challenging.
- **How do the scales feel in or out of balance in the project?** Does something feel off to you in your plot or in the

emotional resonance? Pay attention to how plot lines are going to evolve by asking yourself "What happens if they do that?" play it out in your head and then ask "What if" over and over again until you get to the end? Does it feel right?

- You often have to work twice as hard to earn a happy ending by throwing a lot of crap before the character gets it- our pessimistic natures are more likely to believe a negative coincidence than a positive one. So don't go easy. Trust your gut and check out options as to how the end could go and give it the Justice check before you commit to any outcome.
- Even with memoir, you can modulate this by slowing down for challenges or speeding up as needed to make the payoff feel earned. How much you choose to reveal or conceal in either case can be the difference between a successful ending and one that falls flat.

For the journey of the characters:

- **What is your character hoping to achieve, above all else?** What is the "Justice" they are seeking? What actions are they prepared to take in order to reach their goals? Consider where the scales feel out of alignment, and how they are attempting to right them? Is an accountant who feels underpaid skimming off the reserves of the company? Is a stifled spouse flirting on business trips and getting closer and closer to cheating and headed over the line?

- Being keenly aware of where your characters' lives feel unfair to them will make it MUCH easier to put them in a situation they can't resist so things can get really interesting, but more on that when we reach the Devil.
- For now, it's enough to know where they feel shortchanged and like life owes them something. This could be something you agree with, like a societal wrong that matches your values that they want to correct, or it could be something you find deplorable that they feel they need to do. Either way, all that matters is that it feels like Justice or injustice to them.
- **What choices are your main characters making and how are these choices going to impact their lives?** As an extension of the previous point, how are your characters trying to compensate for what feels unfair in their lives? Or, on the flip side, what are they denying themselves or putting up with because their sense of Justice tells them this is all they deserve?
- Know where your characters' lines in the sand are and then find a plot point or scenario in which they need to step over

those lines and experience the turmoil created by this and you've got a story that will hook both you as you write it and your reader once it's out in the world.

For the project itself:

- **Where are the scales in or out of balance for the piece?** A great way to explore this is through book mapping. Create a spreadsheet for your book, with a row for each chapter. Make a column for each character and major theme in the book. Either make notes on how the theme or character appears in each chapter or leave it blank if it doesn't. This gives a quick visual overview of where the scales are heavy or light. Even more fun? Color code it! (I know the true spreadsheet nerds out there are sighing as I was when I first tried this.

THIRTEEN

The Hanged Man

THE HANGED MAN is one of the cards that people cringe upon pulling from the deck, but I think that, upon close examination, this card could become a favorite. As you can see in the images, the Hanged Man is nearly always pictured as a figure turned upside down. While this can look like a painful experience, or of one in which the figure is trapped, he's rarely ever pictured in a state of struggle. This card is more about a state of surrender that needs to come partway through the journey, especially as you are now past the midway point looking toward the end.

THE HANGED MAN is an important reminder, above everything else. This reminder is twofold: first, that we cannot control everything, nor can we simply power through stuck places and grind to the end of the writing process. At some point, we will get stuck. This card reminds us to surrender and take a breath and enjoy the feeling of hanging upside down for a moment.

The second reminder is that viewing your writing, and your relationship to it, from upside-down is often a good thing to do when you are well into the process. It is not too late at this stage to re-evaluate decisions that you've made up to this point. I had a big Hanged Man moment when I realized that my book needs to be written in 1st person.

Taking a pause and hanging and looking at the story from other angles and then surrendering to things moving more slowly than I would have liked lead to this insight. This week, I encourage you to embody the energy of this card and be open to taking a breath, and being willing to turn your characters' worlds upside down.

TO EXPLORE FURTHER:

- For the Hanged Man, an example of a book that utilizes the Hanged Man concept is *Black Like Me*, by John Howard Griffin. Written in the 1960s, it follows a white American journalist who assumes the identity of an African-American man and writes frankly about how differently he was treated. In an era when people wanted to say equal rights had already happened and anyone who claimed otherwise was being melodramatic, this book turned the perspective on its head and changed the discourse significantly. 50 years after the book was published, articles are still coming out - worth a search and a read to dive in more.

Writing Exercises

After finding balance with Justice, the Hanged Man turns your world, and the book's, upside down. This can be applied in three layers, as always:

For your journey as the writer:

- **What do you need to surrender as the writer of this piece?** A great use of the Hanged Man is to hang out, pardon the pun, with the concept of your piece and turn it over and around in your mind. Imagine explaining it to various people from various parts of your life or to strangers in different circumstances. If any parts of the story are stuck, this process can help you clarify what might not be working for you and potentially reveal the solution.
- **How could you turn your routine or**

way of writing upside down? If you love to outline, try writing a scene by the seat of your pants. If you've been pantsing your book, try an outline for your writing session. Change up the way you write, too: writing by hand if you normally don't, outside if you normally sit indoors, in bed in a notebook if that has previously felt impossible.

- Try surrendering your usual routines this week and see if you find anything new and exciting.

For the journey of the characters:

- **FOR FICTION:**
- **Look at the way your characters act in scenes that aren't quite working. What if they reacted to a situation in a wildly different way or made a different choice?** Try letting go of your assumptions and writing the opposite of what you wrote before, just to see what might happen. Is this new scene more interesting or engaging? Or does it help you see what the original needs because so it can play out as originally intended. Turn it upside down and find some clarity.
- **FOR NONFICTION:**
- **What if you wrote a scene from a different person's point of view OR**

with a different outcome? Write tricky scenes from a different perspective, or write a "what if" scene where the people in the story made different choices. Remember as you write that there is no need to keep this writing in the book, it's just for you to experiment and clarify.

- Sometimes knowing what a person would never do helps you understand why they made the choices they did. Even if you're writing memoir and the person you're writing about is you, it's a different you than you are now, so turning that you on her head can be helpful.

For the project itself:

- **What is the wildest change to this project you can imagine?** Try making a list of the craziest ways you could change this project. Setting it 1,000 years into the future? 200 years in the past? What if your main character was the opposite gender that they now are, but nothing else about the book changed? What if they didn't make an important choice at the beginning of the story – what then?
- See how many wild changes and upside-down turns you can imagine for your project. Do any of them excite you more than what

you have now? If all this exercise does is validate the way the project is currently structured, it will be worth it. Try to come up with at least 20 wild changes. Let's share them in the group. I can't wait to see these!

FOURTEEN

Death

IT IS NOT possible to cheat death. Most importantly, no one will believe in your book if the people inside it cheat death as well. The death card is the card of inevitable consequences. It is not possible for everything to sunshine and rainbows in any story, and Death is needed in order for the sunshine and rainbows to stand out.

THINK of your story as a circle with a dot in the center. That dot is your character and the circle surrounding him or her is their world. In order for a story to succeed, the character must reach the edge of the world as they know it. If it's a big story, like Lord of the Rings, it may take many books and many pages to reach this edge. If it's a more domestic story, you can get to the edge in the length of a short story : Jhumpa Lahiri's collection, *Interpreter of Maladies* is a brilliant example of a smaller circle.

. . .

IN ORDER for your characters to transform, something must die. This doesn't mean that your character herself has to die, but it does mean that she has to experience a death of some kind by the end of the book. Examples of deaths in stories could be the death of a belief, the death of a friendship, the death of a dream. On the flip side, it could also be the death of an expectation your character was living up to that is the turning point. Did your character have pressure on him his whole life to become a doctor, for example, and then did he break away from what his family had prescribed for him, heading off into the unknown to become an artist? There's lots of death here: his role in his family, the death of one path he could have taken, the death of a more obedient self. But this does not have to read like a sad story.

THE MOST CLICHED metaphor for the death card is the caterpillar-into-butterfly image. In order for the butterfly to live, the caterpillar needs to die. In order for your book to end on a satisfying note, you need to know what your character has to lose. If they don' t have anything to lose at all, then the stakes need to be higher. We see this in a particularly obvious fashion in all those Disney cartoons, like Bambi, where the mom dies in the beginning. This is an overused construction, in my opinion, that gets the death out of the way at the beginning so that the rest of the story can be mostly warm and fuzzy.

Let this week be the week you really get into what

your characters have to lose and what they need to let die in order to reach the end.

TO EXPLORE FURTHER:

- Jhumpa Lahiri's *Interpreter of Maladies*, mentioned above.
- Kim Krans, creator of The Wild Unknown, discusses the Death card in episode 31 of the podcast

Writing Exercises

To explore Death's impact on your piece, let's go through our three layers:

For your journey as the writer:

- **What needs to die for you?** Are you trying to accomplish too much in this book? Are there multiple plot lines running all over the place? A frequent issue for writers is trying to do too much in one book. I have talked to numerous clients who have no shortage of ideas and trying to cram them all in is grinding their writing process to a halt.
- Through the Death card, look at which plot lines or characters might need to die in order for the book to live. A word of consolation – they don't need to die forever – you just

might have multiple books on your hands, rather than one as you expected.

- **Are you having trouble allowing Death to touch your characters?** This is a tough one for me. We all get very attached to the people we write about and, especially with fiction, it can be hard to let pain and suffering hit the characters you've come to care so much about. But in order for them to triumph, they need to fall down.
- Look at any places where you've cringed or delayed letting Death reach your characters by making the plot too gentle or easy. What would happen if you didn't protect the people on the page? I expect Death would allow for a more nuanced and dramatic story to emerge.
- Don't hold back from sharing the parts of yourself that needed to die in order to reach the conclusion when writing memoir or nonfiction. This tension and drama is every bit as present in those stories. Let Death in the room and the whole story crackles with life.

For the journey of the characters:

- **Where is Death needed?** As you begin to come to the end of the story, Death needs to be present. Whether this is an actual human or animal who dies, or if it is metaphorical, something needs to die before your story ends. This week, get very clear on what that is. It can be a relationship, a plan, a goal, someone in the story, or an idea among many options.

- Make a list of things that are candidates if you aren't sure what will die before the end and note which ones sizzle with energy as you write them down. These are the ones that will make the ending satisfying.
- **What is your character's relationship to Death?** This is another great character development question. Death isn't always a fearful force. Your character may welcome it. I think in the west in certain cultures we have been brought up to fear death, but this isn't necessarily the case for every person or every situation. Look closely at the relationship to death and loss that each major character in your book has, and see if what you discover surprises you.
- Another valid question is if there's anything your characters wish would die? Are they trying to get away from an expectation, a relationship, a dead-end job, or another situation that just isn't right for them? It's important to remember that people are just as likely to have a hopeful relationship with Death as we do a fear of endings.

For the project itself:

- **What needs to die?** (This may be a question to save until you finish the first draft, but it's one to have in your back pocket for when you get to the end of the story.) Similar to the first consideration for your journey as a writer above, it's worth taking a step back and looking at the piece as a whole, asking if anything needs to die for the book. Are there scenes that just don't work? Kill them off.
- Characters who don't work for you? Those can go, too. No need to kill them violently, you can also just cut them out.
- It's sometimes really hard to cut out parts of a book where you love some of the writing and think about how long it took you to write those sections, but sometimes killing things off makes the whole thing shine. You can use Scrivener to make this process easier for you while you are writing- make a folder in the research section called "CUTS" and cut out the parts you kill off and paste them in there. If you ever find a need for them, then they aren't gone forever, but you will have lightened the book with the force of Death.
- Let Death become your friend and know that cutting a piece down is often the best way to bring it light and air. Death can bring life to your writing, even if it doesn't appear that way at first.

FIFTEEN

Temperance

I'M NOT GOING to lie, Temperance is a card it took me a long time to warm up to. In it, a figure is pictured pouring two cups back and forth into each other. It's a card that speaks of combination, moderation, and opposing elements coming together.

At first, I found this to be a bland experience. But then I was reminded of the following quote from Carl Jung, and this card came to life:

> "The meeting of two personalities is like the contact of two chemical substances: if there is any reaction, both are transformed."

AT THIS POINT in your book, there has been adventure,

the stakes have risen and your character has come close to the edge of his or her (or their) realm of experience. Once a character comes to the boundaries of Fantasia, so to speak, things begin to change.

Temperance is the card that asks you to look at how your character's identity at the beginning of the book will change as we approach the end. Another question, and one I find every bit as interesting, is how will the world around your character change as a result of their having engaged with it? It's important to understand not just how your character is changed by the world, but also how they change the world itself.

BEYOND THIS QUESTION, Temperance asks us to consider the middle way. If your character has veered from one extreme to the other through out the course of the book, how will they find a middle way in the end? We could compare this to a childhood example: if we think of the three beds in the three bears, Temperance is the bed that is neither too hard, nor too soft. It is the one comfortable to sleep in. In this same way, the people in your book may have tried many options, but eventually they must accept one as their final choice. Not every story gets a "just right" like the three bears, but it does find a landing point that is survivable.

TO EXPLORE FURTHER:

- Books that show elements of the Temperance really well:
- *Self-Portrait With Boy* by Rachel Lyon does an excellent job of illustrating both sides of a life-changing choice;
- *My Absolute Darling* by Gabriel Tallent and *The Border of Paradise* by Esme Weijun Wang show characters that are transformed by each other like chemical reactions. Both of these books are quite dark, but beautifully written.
- Esme discussed *Border of Paradise* on the podcast in episode 2.

Writing Exercises

To explore Temperance's impact on your work, let's go through our three layers:

For your journey as the writer:

- **What extremes, if any are you trying to resolve?** Are you feeling conflicted in what your book is about? The genre or the way you want the characters portrayed? Now is the time to look at what extremes you may swing between in your head and find a middle way that works for you. An example from my own writing that I struggle with on an ongoing basis: do I want to pursue traditional publishing for my novel, or do I want to self-publish. I go back and forth on an almost daily basis, but pulling Temperance would make me sit down and weigh the choices back and forth and find a way that worked for me. I would also give myself the advice that, for now, all that matters is writing the best book possible. Once it's done, then that decision can be made. Do you have similar conundrums? Weigh both extremes and see what it might look like to blend the two and find a third way.

- **How has the book changed you? And how has this book been transformed by your writing it, rather than any other writer?** Great books leave a mark on you when you read them, and they definitely transform their writers in the process of being written. All the work, all the thinking, and all the effort that is required in order to write a book changes you. And then this book goes on to change others.
- Take stock when you pull Temperance of how this book has impacted your life. I think you'll be surprised to see the ways your life has been changed by writing. It's also important that this story was written by you. Even if it's your memoir, think about how it's different that you are telling it rather than an outside biographer. It makes a difference that we write books, and it makes a difference to the book who writes it. As an example, just imagine if Silence of the Lambs had been written by Jane Austen instead. It's a fun

exercise to consider- and then think about what makes you unique in your ability to write this book. How has mutual transformation occurred?

For the journey of the characters:

- **What extremes are the people in your book struggling with?** Every character in a book, even if that is a live person in a biography or memoir, struggles with choices. Look at how you can illustrate both sides of the choices that a person has to make. Try to be as fair and complete in the portrayal of both sides as you can, so that the stakes are higher. If the reader really doesn't know which choice a character will make, the ultimate outcome will have both tension and interest.
- **How do the people in you book impact the world around them and each other?** As you are writing, think about your characters and their surroundings and circumstances as chemical substances, just like Jung described. Now that your characters have spent time combining with each other and the world around them, what chemical reactions are starting to happen?
- How will these people never be the same at the end of the story as a result of having encountered each other? This

transformation, if well-considered, leads to an incredibly satisfying finish.

For the project itself:

- **What middle way does the book need to find?** In trying out new perspectives last week with the Hanged Man, you saw new ways of being. Did you find a new POV that brought additional insight to light? Did another character telling the story of the scene bring sizzle and excitement?
- If these explorations with the Hanged Man brought new ideas and experiences to light for the book, Temperance is the point when you decide how to integrate them? Do you need to go back and forth between two points of view? Do you need to show more of the other side of a choice to up the ante? Does the timeline need to jump back and forth rather than proceeding in a straight line? There is always another way to shape the book the way you want to.

SIXTEEN

The Devil

WE ARE NOW FULLY into the section of the Majors that includes "the cards everyone wants to put back in the deck." People don't like pulling Death. Nor the Devil. (Tune in next week for the Tower, the third of the three most dreaded cards going).

So... how can we use the Devil to great effect in our writing? I would argue that it is the card that can give the most depth, interest, and tension to your work. The Devil is not necessarily about a really really bad character, although that is one way it can appear. I am far more interested in its other identities: temptation, the shadow side, and that which is bad for us but we just cannot resist.

THESE ARE the elements that can really sell an ending. Readers don't buy it if the characters in your book remain Pollyanna-pristine and never face the darker side of life. I have always loved the Housewives' Tarot depiction of the Devil as a giant piece of chocolate cake. Because the devil doesn't look like a bad influence if the story is really good. The devil looks like the best lover you've ever seen. He looks like a treat. She looks like something delicious.

AT SOME POINT, the people you write about need to encounter the Devil. They need to screw up and sleep with their neighbor. They need to make a bad decision. They need to blow all their money gambling. This is why we write books. People want to read them and learn. If you're writing a memoir, you don't need to go the A Million Little Pieces route and make up a far more crazy life than you actually lived, you just have to get honest and share the parts about you that are darker and succumbed to temptation. This vulnerability on the part of whoever you write about will give the reader something to hold onto.

The questions I encourage you to consider this week as we hang out with the Devil are about vice, weakness, and where your characters can't resist. This will hopefully give you more optimism when you draw this card and reach this stage in the process.

TO EXPLORE FURTHER:

Great examples of the Devil:

- Humbert Humbert in Lolita

- James Spader in Sex, Lies, and Videotape
- Last Tango in Paris, full stop
- BOB in Twin Peaks
- Gary Oldman as Dracula
- Casanova

Writing Exercises

To explore how The Devil can inform your story and create the best ending:

For your journey as the writer:

- **What temptations are you facing?** A conversation I reference often is this interview with Zadie Smith. She talks about looking back on her early writing and cringing because certain passages felt like lies. Like she took shortcuts and didn't fully get into the truth of the story. She was writing fiction, but I think this applies to both. Where are you tempted by the Devil to take the easy way out? Where could you go back and look closer?
- **Are any of your characters' temptations ones you have trouble facing in yourself?** As we write about

characters and people who have flaws, as all characters and people do, it can sometimes be hard to get inside temptations that we are disgusted by or that aren't temptations we relate to.

- Often in writing villains or antagonists, we can fall into the trap of flattening characters because we don't relate to their weaknesses. A pacifist writer will have trouble with a murderous villain, as a broad strokes example.
- What flaws do you have trouble connecting with? Is there any way you can bridge that gap? It can feel disgusting and awful to get inside the headspace of a deplorable character, especially if it's one you encountered in real life.
- Take your time, go slow, and be gentle with yourself. The more human you can make these dark figures, the more rich your writing will be, so it's worth taking the time to find the humanity inside them.

For the journey of the characters:

- **What is each major character's Achilles heel?** Take some time to sit with each major character in your story and inquire what their biggest weakness is. It could be something more obvious like gambling or alcohol or an addiction that is easier to categorize. But it could also be something less tangible like always needing to be right, perfectionism, gossip, or other things that tear apart the life a person tells themselves they want to live.

- **How can you force the major figures to face their temptation?** As we've discussed the creation of an ending, it's very important that your story forces your character into a situation that tempts them. It could be something small like cheating on a test, telling a lie or it could be as big as murder or an affair.
- The issue is that your character needs to be put in a high-stakes situation before the end of the story and to react to that situation in some way. They can resist, or succumb. There is usually a cost to this choice. Maybe they keep their ethics in place, but lose something else. Macbeth supported his wife, but allowed his king to be killed for his advancement. We can also imagine consequences if he had prevented Lady Macbeth from killing the king and how that would also have changed his life in a different way. There is never an easy answer.

For the project itself:

- **What temptation exists in the world you are writing about?** Beyond what any individual character, there can be a cultural temptation at play. Is this character in a very materialistic culture, and has to work with a societal temptation in addition to her own issues?

- Or is there something everyone is navigating toward that this character then wants to give up, even as the whole culture pushes him in the direction it is invested in?
- Having a wide view on temptation can really add a lot of nuance and sophistication to your story, so dive deep!

SEVENTEEN

The Tower

OH BOY. We have referenced feared cards up to now, but of all the cards people fear pulling, the Tower takes the cake. This is where the shit hits the fan, things fall apart, and that thing has been building toward a point of explosion explodes. I am reminded of a favorite line in the Woody Allen movie, Bullets Over Broadway when the mafia boss is on the phone with his henchman, "Burn it down, Cheech. I want it to look like arson."

In the context of writing, I see the Tower as the climax. All the threads of the story have been building to a point where things come together and transform. And transformation cannot come without destruction in some form or other, even if the result is beautiful. A baby is a beautiful thing, but the birth process is not a peaceful one.

The Tower is labor and childbirth. It's the wildfire that leaves fertile soil behind. It is a house fire, the loss of a job, the end of a relationship, it is the Great Depression, the financial crisis of 2008. It is Enron's collapse. It is an earthquake or a tsunami. This may be a metaphor or an actual event. It is the point when everything comes to a head.

ONE THING to note is that the experience of the Tower feels much more violent to those who resist change. To anyone who clings to the status quo, this upheaval will feel like the end of the world. To others, it may feel like revolution. Which it is can be a worthy exploration in your story.

A final thought- Susannah Conway made the wise comment that in all the images of the Tower she has reviewed generally show the Tower falling apart but the foundation below standing strong. So another way to look at this point is a cataclysmic event that clears out everything in the way of seeing the part of a character or a situation that holds firm. Witness, every disaster/adventure story in which the apocalypse or some other event gets rid of the distraction of petty things and has characters stepping up to do heroic things because nothing else matters anymore. Your story doesn't have to be a superhero narrative to make use of this structure. Let's get into the reflection questions to see how you can apply this concept below.

TO EXPLORE FURTHER:

Books and Films that Utilize the Tower Archetype Successfully to Advance the Plot:

- *The Wizard of Oz*, L. Frank Baum
- *Circe*, Madeline Miller
- *The Road*, Cormac McCarthy

Writing Exercises

To explore how The Tower breaks it down to the "nothing else to lose" level:

For your journey as the writer:

- **What are you trying to protect your characters from?** My personal weakness as a writer is delaying the inevitable for my characters. I once wrote 3 scenes in a row of my main character eating a meal, then stopping in a coffeeshop, then dawdling around all to avoid making her go to a place where there was a scene that involved a painful confrontation.
- Are you trying to protect your characters from the influence of the tower? When you pull the Tower, think about the tough things they need to encounter in your book.

- What are you bracing yourself to write? For me, admitting that I was dreading putting her through hell allowed me to lead my character to the inevitable.
- **How will your character ultimately rise on the other side?** I find it helpful to see the Tower as a means to an end, even if the experience of going through it isn't exactly pleasant.
- In your process journal, think about a few times in your life that have made you who you are, and have given you resources you wouldn't have otherwise, even though you wouldn't wish them on anyone.
- Reflecting on how this might reveal new strengths may help you throw your character (or yourself in a memoir) to the wolves for the Tower moment in your book.

For the journey of the characters:

- **Remember when we made the worst nightmare list?** Now is the time to go back to the worst nightmare list that you made for your main characters and to bring them up against their deepest fears. Couldn't live without their beloved home? Burn it down.
- This is not going to be a "giggling as you write" point in the writing process, unless you are like my brother who, when reading Jaws

as a child, was rooting for the shark. Be prepared for this to be hard.

- Take good care of yourself. Take breaks. Watch a few romantic comedies. Breathe.
- As Diana Gabaldon said in a recent appearance about some fans who told her how much Black Jack Randall, her villain, terrified them, "They haven't realized that I am Black Jack Randall."
- We have to become the Tower ourselves as the writer on the people in the world we have created. This isn't always fun. It's normal to get upset and to find this hard. Almost every writer I've talked to about this does. The antidote is to know something will come of it.
- **How do your characters respond to change?** Look at whether the people in your book are the sort of early adopters who love upheaval and revolution and leap with joy into the unknown? If so, they may love the rush of the Tower. Think of heroes on the battlefield who never quite settle down to everyday life afterward.
- On the other side, is your character a recluse who never steps out of his everyday routine into anything new? What might happen if he was forced outside of those lines. Think of A Curious Incident of a Dog in The Nighttime. If Christopher, the autistic main character, weren't so overwhelmed by the outside world,

the events that forces him out into it to find the truth wouldn't be nearly so enjoyable to read. We love seeing how characters respond to the Tower and who they become as a result.

For the project itself:

- **What needs to fall apart in the plot itself?** The blessing and curse of a good outline is that it leads us neatly from the beginning of the book all the way to the end. But, as we reach the tower, sometimes some pieces that you put in place don't feel quite right. They don't sit well, or they feel too neat to be believable. It's human nature to trust in coincidences that hurt the characters. Ones that too easily benefit them can seem unbelievable.
- Go through your plan for the book and see if the Tower has made its mark enough to convince your reader that fate has really had its way with the world in your book. This doesn't need to be an event in your character's direct life: perhaps the background is apocalyptic. Things set against a backdrop of the Tower can be incredibly powerful.
- Alternatively, the Tower can hit hard at the beginning with the rest of the book a

resolution that comes after. You can be just as creative with this element as with any other in the book.

EIGHTEEN

The Star

THIS IS a favorite card of mine. After the powerful destruction of the Tower wiped everything that was not standing strong away, the Star is the hope that remains. I love this transitional point. It would be too jarring to leap from the tower to the blinding light of the Sun, so we begin in the dark with the Star. It is still night, and still primarily dark, but as the chaos of the Tower retreats, we see a star in the night sky.

This is that moment. It is when little tiny dots of light begin to come through. When there is something to wish for. Something new.

I'M NOT sure if many of you remember a film from the 80s called The Neverending Story? There was a force in a world called Fantasia that was called the Nothing. It was destroying everything in its path because people no longer believed in the magic of that world. Eventually, the Nothing consumed everything but left behind one boy who had read the book about this destruction. He stood with Fantasia's childlike Empress who showed him a tiny star in her hand after everything had been wiped away. He commented on how dark it was.

"In the beginning," she said. "it is always dark."

She then asks the boy to make as many wishes as he can think of, because these wishes will bring Fantasia back to the great glory it was before.

THIS IS what the star is in your book. After the shaky elements have been destroyed, the ending of your story requires that the characters inside it build something new. If they have lost their homes in a storm, they need to learn to dream of a new home. They might leave, they might rebuild, they might band together, or they might all break apart. The Star is the point when your characters start wishing for something new after they have lost something important to them.

The Star is the beginning of mending a broken heart and being ready for a new love. It is realizing that what was lost might not be the thing they wanted most after all. And it can also be the point when you learn who the character really is.

ONE OF MY favorite descriptions of the Star is from Jessa Crispin's book, in which she calls it "The David Bowie card," something the Lioness tarot has clearly taken to heart in the image above. David Bowie wasn't content with being just another rock and roller. He was a Star Man and he wanted everyone to see him sparkle.

Whoever your characters are if they are free to not care what anyone else thinks, is what the Star reveals. This might be something beautiful or something terrible that is discovered, or it might be a terrible beauty that combines them both. Let their brilliant truth and unique selves come to light now. It's time for them to wish new selves into existence.

TO EXPLORE FURTHER:

- *The Neverending Story* Scene referenced above
- Listen to David Bowie while journaling when you pull this card.
- A beautiful documentary that has always embodied the Star for me: *Paris is Burning*, about the drag ball culture

Writing Exercises

To explore how The Tower breaks it down to the "nothing else to lose" level:

For your journey as the writer:

- **What hope do you have for your story now?** After breaking down anything shaky and letting it fall apart last week with the Tower, look at what foundation has been left behind. What does this place look like now without the shaky structures hiding it?
- Who or what is left behind and what can be built on top of this new place. if you had no plan or sense of how this story would end, what would you wish for now?
- **What is twinkling in the dark of your book?** Who have you become, having written all this way? After writing and writing

for months and from building up your characters and stories and then watching them fall down, what hope do you have for them?

- What do you wish as the writer of this story? What dreams do you hold for where they could go, if given the chance? These things may not be slated to come to pass, but you and the reader deserve a breath after all the wildness that has come up to this point.
- Take this moment to dream about where this story could go without worrying whether or not it will. Dream up two or three endings that could happen at this point. Try them on. See how they feel.

For the journey of the characters:

- **Who have your characters become?** Take a page of paper and write a little sketch of each major character and review who they were when you began, what they have been through, and who they have been revealed to be now in all their glory. Perhaps they were innocent, went through hell, and are now bitter and jaded. That could be the foundation you are working from. Or perhaps they are stronger and braver than before.
- Taking a moment to assess what each person

has been through and who they are now can help determine whether or not the final steps to the end will be believable and effective.

- **What is unique about each character?** How is each character you have a Starman or Starwoman? What special stardust do they each have for the world. It could be something very small- they are a good listener or they alone bake the best pie in the land, or it could be something as significant as Frodo, destined to save the world from the ring by throwing back in Mt. Doom.
- Write a few phrases about the stardust each character has to share, so we get to see it in action by the end of the book.

For the project itself:

- **What hope and wishes are present in the story now?** Whether or not they actually come to pass, it's good to know what the reader is hoping for in the story now. If there is a romantic plot, people are probably hoping the lovers come together. There may be a sort of quest that needs to come to the end. Or there may be a goal that a character has been trying to accomplish throughout the book.
- Know what the wish of the story is now, as

you'll need to decide whether it happens and write us through to the end of that wish by the end of the story.

NINETEEN

The Moon

I WON'T LIE, visually, this is a big of an odd duck card, and for good reason. The Star is so clear and twinkly and has an easy visual statement to grasp. When people pull the Moon, the first question always seems to be, "What's up with that Lobster?"

IN TERMS OF CHRONOLOGY, the Star is the moment in the night where you see the first light twinkling before going to bed and everything feels sparkly. The Moon, on the other hand, is when you wake up in the middle of the night with all your fears right in your face. These fears are the lobsters crawling out of the depths of the ocean and, in some decks, the wolves howling out in the dark.

The Moon acknowledges that with big change comes fear. While everything might have felt like ti was on the upswing with the Star, most people have a hard time leaping into action for a new plan. They wonder, "Wait a minute- was this really a good idea?" and start to doubt themselves. All those doubts and unconscious material is the Moon's territory.

Before we get to the Sun and the next morning, the book needs to go through its own Dark Night of the Soul to really be ready to come to the end.

WHEN YOU PULL THE MOON, think of moments of awareness that come in the moments between a big transformational event and what ultimately unfolded afterward. This is that point for your story. Let them see what their fears are, a bit like Alice falling slowly down the well and having time to assess all the items on the shelves.

Once you get to the bottom of the well with the Moon, we'll be ready to take the book out that little door into the Sun next week.

Another thought- this doesn't have to be a scary process for every character or every book. The other influence of the moon is wildness and the howling wolf. This may be a chance when the inner wildness finally gets to come out for someone after they come through a big change- this is a great time to explore what wild howling would look like for your story- let that be something to ponder at this point, too.

TO EXPLORE FURTHER:

- Anything by David Lynch
- *Alice in Wonderland* is a great one to revisit for the Moon- either the book or any of the many movies. Dame Darcy recently released an Alice in Wonderland deck, if you want to fully immerse!
- *Women Who Run with the Wolves* by Clarissa Pinkola Estes is amazing for the wolf archetype – always a favorite. The audio version is divine.

Writing Exercises

To explore how The Moon goes into the depths:

For your journey as the writer:

- **What do your dreams tell you about the project?** The Moon dives into the unconscious, your hopes, fears and what lies beneath. In contrast to the hopes of the Star which are bright in the sky for you to see, the Moon has a quieter voice. Play with writing your dreams down this week and see what they tell you about the book.
- **What lobster are you afraid will crawl out before finishing this draft? Or- what wildness needs to come out** As you can see above, a common motif of the Moon is the lobster crawling out of the ocean. What fears do you have about what

won't work, what won't come together, or any fear at all about the writing- acknowledge them and write about them in your process journal.

- For the wolf side, do some free-writing about what it would look like for the story to really let go and get wild. This part can feel really fun.

For the journey of the people/characters in your piece:

- **What is lurking in the depths of your characters now?** After going through the intensity of all that has come before, leading up to the Tower, characters get shaken up and they change. They may hope things will be different now and see a new course with the Star, but along with that comes fear about what will be different for them- try reflecting on and writing about the deepest fears your characters have NOW after all the events of the book have taken place.
- **Try out a dream sequence?** A joke in the National Novel Writing Month community is that when you can't figure out how to get to your 1,667 words a day because you've run out of things to say, write a dream sequence. This doesn't necessarily have to go in the book, but try writing a dream sequence or –

even better – a nightmare that brings all that's hiding in the shadows to the surface.

- For nonfiction, try writing a scene where all the main figures' worst fears come to pass – this could be the you at that point in the memoir, or any other person who appears in the book as well. This can also be a wild woman/man sequence that lets the wolf side go. Have fun with these!

For the project itself:

- **Has anything significant been left out?** As we come closer and closer to the end, take this card as an opportunity to consider the themes that have been addressed so far. Has anything been left unsaid? Is that ok or do you feel like you are avoiding something. This is the moment to pay attention to the little voice that is saying "but what about...?"
- If there are nagging feelings that something needs to be considered, take time to explore those elements now.
- You can make decisions about what's included and what's not in revision, but the first draft is for looking under every stone that calls to you. Go looking for your lobsters and howling wolves this week!

TWENTY

The Sun

AFTER DIVING INTO THE DEPTHS, the pain, and the shadows and having just a glimmer of hope, it is now here when you draw the Sun. All metaphors about light apply with this card: the lights are now on, things are now clear in the light of day, and warmth has returned. Whereas with the Moon, there can by a mysterious feeling and a swimmy dream logic that dictates the storyline, the Sun is straightforward and absent of deception. If the Moon was a David Lynch movie, the Sun is more like a summer blockbuster or a romantic comedy: what you see is what you get.

I KNOW some of you will feel relief at this shift, while others will worry about this experience being too banal or boring. Fair enough- a fun way to play with the Sun is to consider the tension between what the character believes is the Sun, ie straightforward, obvious and objectively true; and what is actually the Sun. It's just as interesting witnessing someone getting the Sun wrong as it is seeing someone reach a long overdue realization.

The metaphor of the lightbulb coming on also fits here- what realizations has your character come to at this point? Perhaps even more importantly, what conclusions does the reader need to reach?

The Sun is the time when you, as the writer, get to decide what will be resolved (Sun) and what will remain mysterious (Moon). The best endings have a bit of each polarity. We crave the satisfaction of knowing "what happened??" as readers, but we also find it more satisfying when things aren't all perfectly tied up with a bow on them.

A FUN CONCEPT I want to bring up is the Johari Window, which you may or may not be familiar with.

HERE IS A VISUAL OVERVIEW:

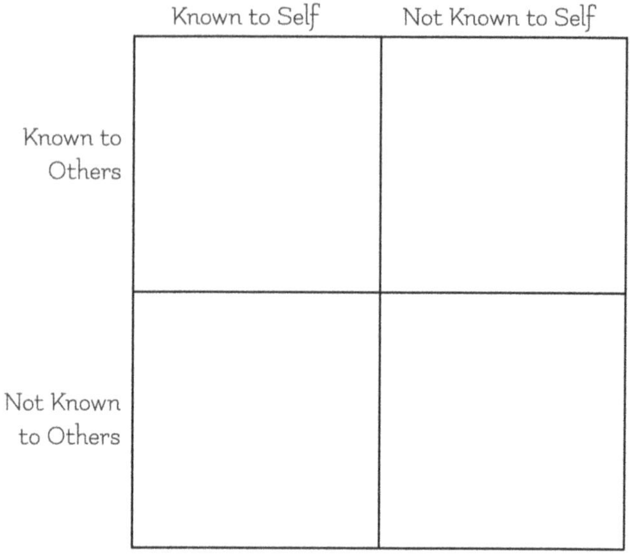

This is a helpful concept to explore in connection with your characters and in connection with the Sun. The Sun is where there is light, in other words where something is known.

The top left part of this diagram is the Sun: things that are obvious to everyone. Examples include, a character's physical appearance for the most part: what color hair they have and eye color and how tall they are. They know this about themselves (unless they can't see) and other people in the story know it about them as well.

Things in the bottom left are more in the shade: things that the character knows but others don't. This might include, dreams or fears they have, hidden agendas, and secrets.

Top right is things not known to the character, but

that other people know, also a bit in the shade. This might include a character who has feelings for someone but has convinced themselves that they don't. Or characters with mental illness who believe things that other people can see aren't objectively true. This could also be things characters have gotten wrong about themselves, like body dysmorphia or believing they are unlovable while others find them charming, or the opposite.

Finally, the bottom right is things that are unknown to the character as well as everyone else, such as what will happen in the future, how events will ultimately end up, unseen consequences and so on- this is all the way out of the Sun's light and entirely unconscious.

TO GIVE YOU ADDITIONAL CONTEXT, I have broken out cards from the major arcana and how they might fit into this window as a reference:

	Known to Self	Not Known to Self
Known to Others	Sun The Empress The Emporer The Chariot	The Heirophant Strength The Devil
Not Known to Others	The Magician High Priestess The Hermit	The Fool Wheel of Fortune Hanged Man Death The Tower

We could probably have a lively debate about whether or not these delineations fit- some cards can work in more than one box.

A fun exercise is to play with what the Sun is shining on by drawing a Johari Window and then pulling a card for each square to assess what is known and what isn't for your character. This is especially helpful when working with POV.

TO EXPLORE FURTHER:

- Of course, listen to Here Comes the Sun, both the classic Beatles version as well as Nina Simone's, my personal favorite.

Writing Exercises

To explore how The Sun shines its light:

For your journey as the writer:

- **What is known to you about your project?** Write "What I now know" at the top of a sheet of paper and then free write what is out in the light about your project. Try going for 5-10 minutes, with a timer. Every time you get stuck, start the next sentence with "I know…"
- **What do you want to be resolved at the end of the story?** Take some time to assess what you think needs to be resolved in the end and what you plan to leave in the shadows. A simple way to do this in your process journal is to draw a vertical line and split the page in two with "Resolved" at the top of one column and "Unresolved" at the

top of the other. See how it feels in your body to write things in each column – start with pencil – and then work your way through the elements of how you expect or plan for things to end.

For the journey of the characters:

- **Try the Johari window exercise above.** Draw the quadrant and then make short notes in each square to assess what they now know, what it unknown to them and known to others and so on through the diagram. This can help clarify the ending a bit – a question to consider is if things are going to move from one box to another? Play with various plot developments that would create a shift of squares. Examples:
- Something unknown to everyone becomes known to the character in an a-ha moment (bottom right to bottom left)
- Something unknown to everyone becomes known to the character and the world (bottom right to top left)
- The character comes to understand what only others knew about them (top right to top left)
- People find out something the character was concealing from everyone (bottom left to top left)

- Come up with others on your own, or get crazy and plan some two step shifts.
- **Write a synopsis.** This is a good point to write out the details of the plot and what happens from an objective point of view. If you were going to tell someone exactly what happens in your book play by plat with no need to conceal anything for the sake of spoilers, what would you say happens? Having this clarity of the Sun can help as you get to the end of a first draft.

For the project itself:

- **Does your book have anything to tell you?** Just as our characters have blind spots, we as writers may be missing something in our projects due to our own limited access. Let your book speak by doing some free-writing.
- At the top of a blank page write "What I wish [Your Name] understood" and then write from the point of view of your story, which wants to be understood and told. Try this with a timer for 5 minutes, and if you get stuck start again with "I also wish [NAME] understood..." and continue. See what new things come into the light of the Sun.

TWENTY-ONE

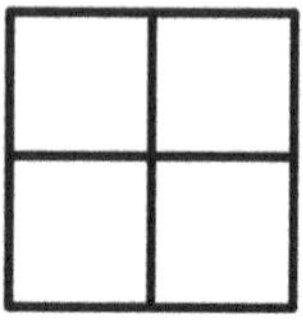

Judgement

A CARD with a scary sounding name to be sure, Judgement isn't the battle-axe its name makes it out to be. Judeo-Christian context is constantly threatening what will come on the day of Judgement, but if we boil it down, all Judgement is for is to take the time to determine what the impact of the journey has been. After assessing what has come to pass in the bright light of the Sun last week, Judgement takes the process a step forward and asks "what next?"

As your characters come to the end, and you've considered what will be wrapped up and what will be left unresolved from the Sun last week, now it's time to put those storylines in place. If the Sun was getting clarity on which storylines to tie up, Judgement is how you do so. Judgement is resolution and taking steps forward after everything has come to light. It's people deciding where to go next. It's a fresh start and figuring out what this whole process meant.

In addition, if your characters have made mistakes, have regrets, or behaved in a way they are less than proud of, this is the time to assess the impact these poor choices have made and to attempt to make amends. It's a time for reflection. This time of year, we are surrounded by graduation ceremonies for schools at all levels from the youngest to the most advanced students. I think of Judgement as a sort of graduation. This part of the adventure is coming to an end, and now it's time to look at what has been learned and where the next steps will lead.

To Explore Further:

Writing Exercises

What to ponder and explore for Judgement:

For your journey as the writer:

- **How will you leave the characters at the end?** If you've pulled the Sun, you decided what elements to leave unresolved and which need to be tied up and sorted out. When you pull Judgement, think about how these events will unfold. Have a love story that's getting a happy ending? Think about how. Is your character going to throw something away and waste an opportunity? Start connecting dots from the idea to what actually happens.
- **What do you need to know in order to write the end?** Not every bit of information you discover or seek out about the book will end up on the page, but there is

often a bit of clarification that needs to happen at this point- perhaps even puzzling out what may happen outside the confines of the book itself.

- Do you need to know how some characters will end the rest of their lives in order to get clear on where the ending of the book lands?
- Write out bullet points to get clear on those events. Give yourself space to free-write alongside the book's contents so you can clarify all the context you need to in order to sort out the ending.

For the journey of the characters:

- **What do they need to end the book?** This is a great dialogue exercise to do in your process journal. For each major character, find two different colored pens and ask them questions you need the answers to in order to wrap up. Some ideas of what to ask:
- What do you need me to know as we come to the end?
- What is most important to you that the reader know about your experience?
- What would you prefer to keep secret?

- **Let them tell their autobiography.** This is a variation on the option above. Let your main characters tell you what happens the rest of their lives after the end of the book. This may be easier than trying to "come up with it" per the option above.

- If you prefer to listen to the characters and have them show what comes next and take your lead from them directly, this will be an easier option. In your process journal or on a blank piece of paper, ask a character, "So what happened next?" and let them tell you where things went until the end for them.
- Knowing where the end is for them can help you decide where to end the book. It's also fair to ask the characters where they think the story ends.

For the project itself:

- **When does the end occur?** Having done the explorations above, it's time to decide when the book ends. Just as we often write some "throat clearing" portions of a story and then realize the book actually begins at a later point, placing the ending point is another challenge that can happen once you have clarity from the exercises above. Knowing when in the chronology the end comes and what will be resolved vs what will be left to the imagination will help you arrive at the finish line in a satisfying way.

TWENTY-TWO

The World

WE BEGAN WITH THE FOOL, beginning the draft and taking steps forward into the unknown. Now the journey is complete, and the work must find its way into the world. The characters have progressed through the obstacles and have succeeded or failed, we have changed as writers going through the process and now this incarnation of the stages of the story is over.

THE WORLD MEANS TWO THINGS, in my view: both that the inner transformation that has happened between the Tower and Judgement now needs to be connected with the outside world.

The insights gained must be shared, and the awareness will only benefit the world if it touches others. So the character needs to go off into the sunset, as we always see in formulaic Western films. It's time to conclude this tale and move on to the next one.

On the second level, the manuscript you have written through this cycle of the Major Arcana needs to be shared with the world. It's time for you to complete this draft and begin another one. Or, if further along, it's time to share it with part of the world (an editor or other support team member like an agent or proofreader) or the world (by publishing the project, either on your own or with a publishing house.)

ONCE WE GET to the World a cycle is complete. It may not all be completely wrapped up in a bow with everything working out perfectly, but the story does now fade back into the rest of the world.

Whenever I finish reading a book, I have the sense of the divide between the rest of the world that my life inhabits and the focused world of the book that I've been living inside while reading it. And once I get to the last page, there is a blurring and merging. I carry the parts of the book I loved most with me, but the story is no longer the boundary of the book. I've brought those bits back with me into the rest of my world and now those parts of the book I remember move forward as I step back into the Fool and begin again.

Eventually the story has to leave the nest. The World represents sharing our words with all the readers out there who are looking for a story that carries them away on an adventure or a process that will help them learn and discover something new.

Writing Exercises

What to ponder and explore for the World:

For your journey as the writer:

- **Who needs to see your project now?** When pulling the World, there are a active steps to take. The first is to set the story aside for a time. At least a couple of weeks. You can work on other writing, take a break, or take on something entirely different to refill yourself creatively.
- If you've gotten to the end of your draft, take at least a couple of weeks before returning to the pages to review. Come back with fresh eyes. This will not happen overnight. In addition to your fresh eyes coming to the page, consider who else you would like to have read it:
- An editor?

- Potential agent?
- Beta readers?
- Writing group?
- Trusted friend or family member? (choose these very carefully, as this can get tricky)
- Proofreader? (If you're almost finished with the book and ready to move forward to publication)
- **What do you need in order to release this story to the world?** Even submitting a book for consideration to an agent, a contest, a publisher, or an editor takes courage and can bring up lots of fears.
- Consider what you need in order to let the book more forward to where it will take up more space in the world and where eyes other than your own will see the story.
- Do you need to journal? Light a candle for your writing self? Have a party with friends to celebrate getting to the end of your draft?
- Treat yourself to acknowledge work well done so you can move forward with a sense of freedom as the next stages of the process will feel very different than when you were writing.

For the journey of the characters:

- **How will they move off into the sunset?** Now it's time to say goodbye to your characters as they make their exits.

Most likely, they will continue their lives after the book ends.

- Even if your main character's entire life is contained within the book, there are some characters who will move off the page and back into their own worlds.
- Take your time and say goodbye to them as they go. This may be hard, so give yourself time and space as you wave goodbye.

- **Are there any last secrets they want to tell you?** This information may be hidden from the reader, but if you need some closure with any of your characters it is worth asking if they have anything else they need to tell you.
- You can journal back and forth with them in different colors, or do a meditation where you sit down with them and visualize them in a chair opposite to you and ask them if there is anything else they need you to know in order to tell the end of their story properly.
- Ask them if they prefer that these discoveries remain secret or if they would prefer that it was shared – however you feel best proceeding.

For the project itself:

- **What is the next step?** As discussed above, reaching The World means that there is a leap into the unknown with The Fool around the corner. This could be the next draft, or it could be letting the book go out into the world by publishing.

- That experience of the book being released can turn into its own Major Arcana journey, ending with the Fool again as you contemplate another book... Consider where you go next with this story so it continues to move closer and closer to getting out in the world.

Congratulations! You've reached the end of the Story Arcana cycle. Whether you worked through these prompts one by one or drew cards at random to work your way through, drawing The World is an indicator of reaching the end of the cycle.

Even if this is the very first card you drew in the process, take a moment to reflect on all that you've accomplished with your writing. Your current book may not yet be finished, but many goals you've set in life have been accomplished.

Remember a time you completed something momentous when you draw the world. Close your eyes and let that feeling sink in. You will reach that point with your writing.

It is possible. Keep going. Your story is worth it.

Appendix

Spreads for writing

In creating my course, Story Arcana, I wanted to show a way that tarot spreads could create deeper exploration and discovery for writers. That course serves as a companion to this book and reveals additional material and resources. I've included two spreads from the course below for your reference:

Dialogue:

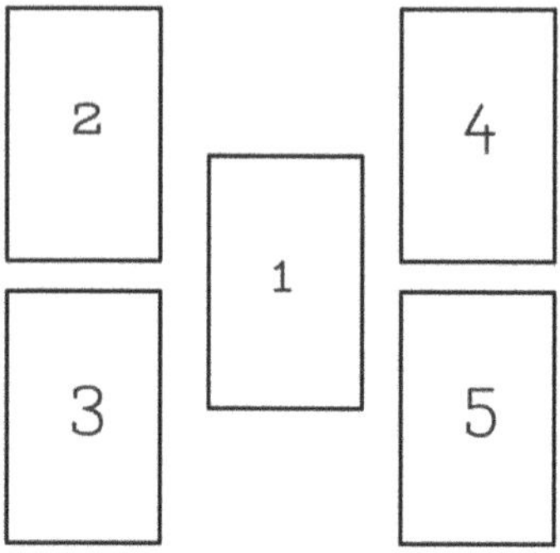

1. The conversation.
2. Character 1.
3. C1 Unspoken agenda.
4. Character 2.
5. C2 unspoken agenda.

Each of these spreads illustrates how you can pull cards to dive deeper into a situation. In the first spread above, pull a card for each of the characters in a conversation you are writing. You can expand this spread to include as many characters as you like- simply have the character cards radiate around the conversation card and you can place the card representing what's underneath next to the character card.

Often what makes dialogue effective, interesting and natural is the fact that people almost never say what they mean, and conversations are never about what they appear to be on the surface. A couple discussing whether or not they need to buy more milk isn't really talking about the milk, or the scene doesn't need to be in your book:

"We need milk," she said.

"Great," he replied. "I'll pick some up on the way home. Thanks for reminding me!"

Yuck. This is going to be the first scene on the cutting floor.

If, however, she's asking him to get milk, but really she's worried he's having an affair, there's more to dig in to. Especially if he's actually lost his job but doesn't want his wife to know yet:

"Hey - we're out of milk. What are you doing this afternoon?"

"Well, I actually had something happening. Can I check in later?"

"Really? You never said. I was really hoping to have it for tonight. Are you going to be late?"

"I hope not, but you never know, right?"

"I see," she said.

If your conversations are feeling too "on the nose" try this spread to get to the subtext that's lurking underneath. You might find some crazy motivations and urges you never knew your characters were having.

The Hero(ine)'s Journey:

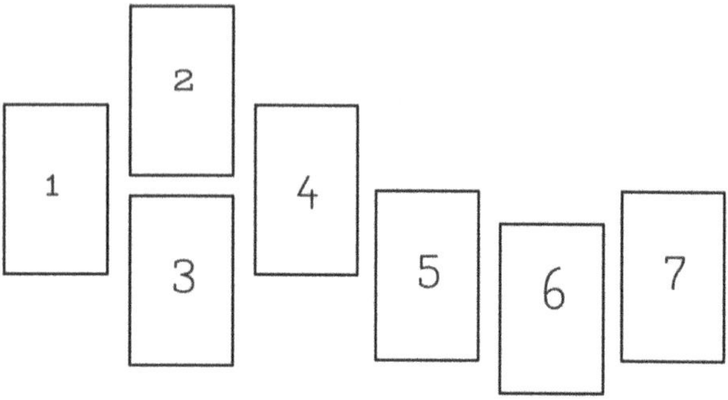

1. Character at the beginning.
2. Fears.
3. Aspriations.
4. Synthesis.
5. Getting down to business.
6. Recognition.
7. Reversal & final point.

This is a great one to try when you are mapping out the full span of what the character is going to accomplish in the course of your book. Also great to use for their lifetime and then narrowing down which part of it you want to include in the story.

Characters need to transform throughout the course of the narrative, so you can use this spread to see where they are at the beginning (Card 1) the series of things that transform them (cards 2-6) and then what the resolution is for them at the end (card 7).

The basic overview of this spread is to pull a card for the character (1) then for what they fear most (2) and what the best possible outcome they are seeking is (Aspirations, 2) and the way these two dynamics combine for them (4). Card 4 is a great way to see if their fears or best self is winning- does card 4 more resemble 2 or 3?

Next, look at what happens when they begin to seek their goals (or avoid them) in earnest as the book gets down to business (5). To use Aristotelian lingo, the recognition (6) is when everything comes to a head and the character sees where things are headed in the end and then we can see how this transforms them into someone new in the reversal. (7). For tarot readers, this reversal has nothing to do with pulling a card upside down, it's just the reversal of the plot, where the events unfolding cause the character to change their direction in some way.

If this sort of spread is of interest to you, Story Arcana the course is a self-paced course available to you at any time. You can learn more about the course and sign up here:

carolinedonahue.com/storyarcana

Decks I love

If you're buying a deck for the first time, the most important thing is that the art is appealing and enjoyable to look at for you. Since using it with writing is done in order to connect to your subconscious first, it is even more essential that the art in your deck delights you. Don't worry about getting the right one. If you love your deck, it's right for you and no one's greatest hits list - including mine - should keep you from getting a deck that is calling your name. By the same token, you may hate all the decks listed below if you have different taste that mine. That's ok- follow your heart as they are so many decks out there now. There is one for everyone these days.

Trying to choose a favorite deck - or even three favorite decks - was just too painful, so here are the decks I use most frequently from my gigantic and obsessive tarot collection. Before purchasing a deck, I highly recommend seeing it in person, if possible, if you have a store nearby that has sample decks you can view.

As some of these decks are independently produced by artists and not always in stores, at a minimum I recommend seeing as many images of the cards as you can before buying. I've had it happen more than once that I fall in love with one image only to receive the full deck and find that first card is the only one that speaks to me.

Online image searches as well as the site **aeclectic.net/tarot** are great resources to see a wide variety of images from a deck before buying. Many decks have their own sites that show a full array of card images as well. Finally, quite a few decks have been made into apps, which is an inexpensive way to take a test drive of a deck before committing to the physical one - also a great way to pull a card on the go.

Here is a list of my most-used decks:

The Aquarian Tarot
The Bohemian Gothic Tarot
The Botticelli Tarot
Circo tarot
Dame Darcy Mermaid Tarot
The Dreaming Way tarot
The Ghetto Tarot
The Fountain Tarot
The Housewives' Tarot
The Japaridze Tarot
Kat Black's Golden Tarot
The Light Grey Tarot

Light Visions (Two color version of Prisma Visions)
The Lioness Oracle Tarot
The Mary-El
Mesquite tarot
Moon Child Tarot
Nomad Tarot
Pagan Otherworlds Tarot
Persephone Tarot
Prisma Visions (Full Color version of Light Visions)
The Silent Tarot
Slow Holler
Small Spells Tarot
Starchild Tarot
Starved City Tarot
Stella's Tarot
The Wild Unknown
The Wooden Tarot

Recommended Reading and Resources

Should you wish to work more in depth with tarot and your writing, here are a few final resources:

I work with clients 1:1, offering Literary Tarot readings. If you'd like to book one for yourself, you can do so here: https://carolinedonahue.com/literary-tarot-readings/

The course, Story Arcana, is a companion to this book and explores more spreads and specific examples on how to use tarot to support your writing. Two spreads from that course appear in the appendix. You can learn about the course and sign up here:

https://carolinedonahue.com/storyarcana/

In addition, I can recommend the following books on tarot:

21 Ways to Read a Tarot Card by Mary K. Greer
The Creative Tarot by Jessa Crispin
Kitchen Table Tarot by Melissa Cynova
A Magical Course in Tarot by Michelle Morgan

Modern Tarot by Michelle Tea

Tarot 101 by Kim Huggens

The Tarot Coloring Book by Theresa Reed

Tarot for Life by Paul Quinn

Tarot Plan and Simple by Anthony Louis

Tarot Wisdom by Rachel Pollack

Several Courses I love if you really want to get into the cards:

Daily Guidance and 78 Mirrors by Susannah Conway, available at susannahconway.com

The Little Red Tarot shop out of the UK had some lovely courses, currently closed for registration, but you can get on their list at littleredtarot.com to learn when they'll next be open.

Enjoy discovering the tarot and bringing it into your writing. I hope very much that you'll reach out to connect and share your adventures. I'm @carodonahue on Twitter and Instagram. Tag me and #StoryArcana-Book to share your explorations. I can't wait to see!

About the Author

Caroline Donahue is a writer, writing coach, and podcast host living in Berlin. She is the co-editor of the anthology, *I Wrote it Anyway*, and the creator and host of The Secret Library Podcast. She holds a Masters Degree in Psychology and Expressive Arts.

She has been reading tarot since 1996 and has been offering Literary Tarot Readings for writers since 2016. She is currently at work on her first novel.

Visit her online at carolinedonahue.com

facebook.com/thesecretlibrary

twitter.com/carodonahue

instagram.com/carodonahue

Lightning Source UK Ltd.
Milton Keynes UK
UKHW020639221221
396077UK00010B/616

9 780578 455754